END

The book "HOW TO CREATE WEALTH AND PREVENT POVERTY" is a powerful panacea to financial ignorance and penury. It has been carefully researched by a man with an in-depth knowledge in financial management and practice. The classical principles discussed herein can be applied easily by anyone who desires change and quick growth in his/her finances. It is not only a must read for anyone who wants to accelerate accomplishment in personal finance and wealth creation but should serve as a valuable gift to loved ones. The wise instruction you are prepared to take today determines the glorious future you create.

Ambassador Tony Ewelike
Managing Director
AGHomes Ltd, Lagos

HOW TO CREATE WEALTH AND AVOID POVERTY is like a pocket road map to wealth creation! The nuggets of wisdom in this book cannot be fully appropriated at one reading! I pray many people will read this book and practice the principles in it! I intend to read it a few more times!

Pastor Ade Sobanjo
Overcomers Assembly

How to Create Wealth and Avoid Poverty is about taking responsibility for your financial affairs and creating enduring wealth in a Godly manner. If you want all insider wisdom on how to create wealth and avoid poverty, read this book.

It is easy to read and its key messages are very simple. This is the kind of book you buy and give your kids and young school leavers desirous of financial freedom.

It is common sense that might not be common for your financial future.

Tunde Adaramaja FCA
Managing Partner/CEO,
TAC Professional Services (Chartered Accountants) Member of Integra International

---

This book on how to create wealth and avoid Poverty is another masterpiece from the staple of ADEBOLA Olubanjo. It is in line with his life mission of helping all those willing to live fulfilling lives under God. His treatment of the subject is comprehensive and written in a manner that should make for easy comprehension and application. What is more, the book is highly motivating that even those who are already wealthy will still learn a lot from the book. His treatment of how to sustain wealth creation and how to perpetuate it in the family is amazing and I strongly recommend this wonderful book to all who want to fulfil their purpose and destiny on Earth.

Mazi Sam Ohuabunwa OFR,MON
Past Chairman, Nigerian Economic Summit Group.

Endorsement of the book : How to Create Wealth and avoid Poverty

It is indeed with excitement that I write to endorse this wonderful and time relevant book on wealth creation written by my beloved Dr Olubanjo. I am excited about the book because it provides a much needed basis and platform for understanding and engaging the secrets of wealth creation and more so at a time this understanding is most relevant especially in our environment.

First of all the book excites me because it addresses certain key fallacies which have contributed to the poverty trap. These fallacies are firstly the idea that wealth creation is an unfathomable mystery, secondly that wealth is an element of luck and thirdly that wealth cannot be sustained. These fallacies are addressed comprehensively in the book while providing an effective platform for entering into the act of wealth creation.

Secondly the manner of writing and the obvious experience and passion of the author comes across in a simple and clear manner enabling easy communication and therefore assimilation for the readers in a highly practical manner.

And thirdly the book provides a total man i.e. Spirit soul and body approach to this issue effectively providing a comprehensive approach including dealing with the spiritual issues which so easily ambush persons on the journey of wealth creation.

Finally I can guarantee that this book will not only bless the reader but provide a launch pad on the journey to help the reader begin an effective growth on the path of wealth creation.

Adetokunbo Uchechi Obayan
National Vice President Capacity Building FGBMFI Nigeria

Endorsement of the book : How to Create Wealth and avoid Poverty

The content expressed in this book confirms Dr Olubanjo's area of expertise. The simplicity of his writing style transformed my reading experience to a financial evaluation.

Depending on your understanding of wealth creation, you will be either challenged or encouraged to do more."

Thanks again for sharing years of experience to us. It's a blessing.

Jean Ives
Pastor, Overcomers Assembly
Montreal, Canada.

ENDORSEMENT: DR. ADEBOLA OLUBANJO

I have known Dr. Adebola Olubanjo for more than thirty years as a man of dignity and integrity. He will not say what he does not know or mean, talk less of putting into writing. He is a successful man but he conducts himself with modesty and he is very prudent in managing his wealth, his time and words. His enormous wealth of experience as a notable chartered accountant, founder and managing director of a reputable audit firm, financial entrepreneurship consultant and his personal experience and testimony bear eloquent testimony to the lucidity of this book.

PASTOR BOLA ADAMS, Barrister and Solicitor;
Founder, Bola Adams Foundation

How to
CREATE WEALTH
and
AVOID POVERTY

Simple and Practical Tips to
Riches and **Wealth**

ADEBOLA OLUBANJO

WESTBOW
PRESS®
A DIVISION OF THOMAS NELSON
& ZONDERVAN

Copyright © 2016 Adebola Olubanjo.

All rights reserved. No part of this book may be used or reproduced by any means, graphic, electronic, or mechanical, including photocopying, recording, taping or by any information storage retrieval system without the written permission of the author except in the case of brief quotations embodied in critical articles and reviews.

This book is a work of non-fiction. Unless otherwise noted, the author and the publisher make no explicit guarantees as to the accuracy of the information contained in this book and in some cases, names of people and places have been altered to protect their privacy.

Scripture taken from The Living Bible copyright © 1971 by Tyndale House Foundation. Used by permission of Tyndale House Publishers Inc., Carol Stream, Illinois 60188. All rights reserved. The Living Bible, TLB, and the The Living Bible logo are registered trademarks of Tyndale House Publishers.

Scripture taken from the Holy Bible, NEW INTERNATIONAL VERSION®. Copyright © 1973, 1978, 1984 by Biblica, Inc. All rights reserved worldwide. Used by permission. NEW INTERNATIONAL VERSION® and NIV® are registered trademarks of Biblica, Inc. Use of either trademark for the offering of goods or services requires the prior written consent of Biblica US, Inc.

WestBow Press books may be ordered through booksellers or by contacting:

WestBow Press
A Division of Thomas Nelson & Zondervan
1663 Liberty Drive
Bloomington, IN 47403
www.westbowpress.com
1 (866) 928-1240

Because of the dynamic nature of the Internet, any web addresses or links contained in this book may have changed since publication and may no longer be valid. The views expressed in this work are solely those of the author and do not necessarily reflect the views of the publisher, and the publisher hereby disclaims any responsibility for them.

Any people depicted in stock imagery provided by Thinkstock are models, and such images are being used for illustrative purposes only. Certain stock imagery © Thinkstock.

ISBN: 978-1-5127-2527-8 (sc)
ISBN: 978-1-5127-2528-5 (hc)
ISBN: 978-1-5127-2526-1 (e)

Library of Congress Control Number: 2015921455

Print information available on the last page.

WestBow Press rev. date: 02/19/2016

Also by Adebola Olubanjo

- *Vision: Your Bridge to a Better Future*
- *How to Finance Your Business*
- *14 + 1 Things to Improve Your Success in Life*
- *Secrets to Make Your Business Prosper and Prevent Failure*

This book is dedicated to the Almighty God, who alone gives power to make wealth. It is also dedicated to all my readers who aspire to make wealth by the grace of God.

> A persistent person can cook
> a stone and make it soft.
>
> — African Native Adage

Contents

Foreword xv
Preface xvii
Acknowledgements xix
Introduction xxiii
Chapter 1: My Story 1
Chapter 2: Why You Need to Create Wealth 7
Chapter 3: What Hinders Wealth Creation? 11
Chapter 4: You Need a Vision: Your Bridge to a Successful Future 17
Chapter 5: Establish Goals 26
Chapter 6: Hints on Lifestyles that Will Enhance
            Accumulation of Wealth 34
Chapter 7: Strategies for Wealth Creation 38
Chapter 8: Rules for Wealth to Guide Parents and Their Children 60
Chapter 9: How to Stay Wealthy 64
Chapter 10: Wealth: Daily Advice from Great Minds 71
Chapter 11: Conclusion 88
Bibliography 91

Foreword

This book comes at a most appropriate time as many countries are going through changes and transformations, we need to change our individual value system and transform our lives from a mentality of poverty to one of prosperity.

Dr Olubanjo is a chartered accountant and an erudite tax consultant. When he talks about money and wealth creation, you would be wise to listen. He has a wealth of experience from covering years of national and international service in money management in both the private and public sectors.

We are created in the image of God. Therefore, success and prosperity are our birthright. Poverty is a curse; it turns a potential landlord to a perpetual tenant. Poverty reduces a princess to a prostitute. Nothing diminishes a person's self-confidence and self-esteem like poverty. If you see poverty on the highway, you must maintain a good distance from it.

The author teaches us various strategies to acquire and sustain wealth. The first step is self-identity. You must know who you are in Christ. "Therefore if any man is in Christ he is a new creature, old things have passed away behold everything has become new" (2 Corinthians 5: 17 KJV). Poverty feeds on ignorance. When you have an understanding of who God created you to be, you will confront poverty headlong, and it will never come your way again.

Also, you must discover God's purpose for your life. The discovery of purpose is the pathway to prosperity, happiness, and fulfilment. Everyone is created for a purpose. The tragedy of life, though, is that many have failed to release their potential for the benefit of mankind.

The author gives thirty-one capsules, one for each day of the month. As you swallow and digest each capsule, you will discover new opportunities for wealth creation. Your life will not remain the same in the name of Jesus.

It is good to pray for spiritual guidance, but prayer must be supported with meticulous planning and hard work. Dr Olubanjo has emphasized the need for planning your time, income, expenditures, and other resources daily or weekly. You must draw up your to-do list on a regular basis. Opportunities do not knock anymore. You must know how to identify them. There is no substitute for hard work. You must take care of your health by eating properly and exercising regularly.

This book is a must read for those who want to succeed in life. I strongly recommend it to you and your loved ones. God bless you in the name of Jesus.

Charles Aladewolu
President and CEO
School for Business Success
Lagos, Nigeria

Preface

This book is written to inspire you. It caters for those who want to build personal wealth. If you have started on the path to wealth accumulation, this book will enhance your skills and accelerate the process of becoming wealthy and happy. If you are yet to start (or you need more insight on how to accumulate wealth), this book will give you tips to get you out of poverty. It will direct your path into wealth, so you can begin to fully live the life God planned for you. There is no doubt that it is a motivational and teaching book. The book is a natural follow-up to the talks I have given on the subject. Because these talks have proven helpful to so many, I decided to commit the thoughts behind them to writing. The style is deliberately simple. Everyday language is used so that the book can appeal to readers across a broad spectrum.

There are multiple purposes to this book:

- To motivate people to take steps to create wealth for themselves and their loved ones;
- To rally people to avoid poverty;
- To provide a tool for teaching people to begin to create and accumulate wealth;
- To show people how to maintain wealth;
- To show parents how to ensure that their children create wealth as well as maintain and multiply the wealth in their possession;
- To motivate every person to do something to make him- or herself and all around the world live above the poverty level, regardless of age, environment, and country;

- To make every person on earth to cooperate with the creator, the Almighty God, in the work of creation and multiplication of wealth; and
- To demystify the process of wealth creation and accumulation.

If, after reading this book, you are inspired to take a step and begin the journey of wealth creation, the book has achieved its purpose. See you at the top, wealthy, healthy, and happy.

Acknowledgements

I will like to acknowledge all my clients who have given me the opportunity for more than three decades to serve them as they accumulated wealth. In the process of serving you, I have learned the strategies for creating wealth, and my life has changed. Thank you for making me your friend over all these years.

The teachers and authors who made it possible for me to acquire the knowledge I am sharing are deeply appreciated. Without you, my knowledge would have been limited.

I acknowledge my parents who inculcated in me the principles of wealth accumulation from childhood, when my little brain could not fully comprehend the treasure being implanted in my heart. The seeds you planted in me and my siblings have germinated, and they are bringing forth great fruits. Thank you, Dad and Mum.

The Full Gospel Business Men's Fellowship International (FGBMFI) and its members worldwide are acknowledged for the unlimited avenues to share my experience and knowledge. You laid the foundation for me to write this book. Thank you, indeed.

The Council of Foursquare Men (CFM) is duly acknowledged for giving me a chance to serve and develop the skills of great use to me today in the area of wealth accumulation and management. I give special thanks to Bro Churchill, the National President of Council of Foursquare Men (CFM), and all the past presidents for the recognition of talents and promotion of the dignity of men as breadwinners.

I acknowledge my colleagues, past and present, at Adebola Sobanjo & Co. Over the years, we have used some of the principles in the book, and they worked for us. Thank you for believing in me to lead in the process of building a company that is made up of great and potential leaders.

My children and my wife have stayed with me as I made use of some of the principles in this book. You did not always enjoy my decisions, but all the same, you showed me love and care. You have some of the principles in your lives already, and it has yielded good results. Thank you, Ademola, Oluwaseun, Olufemi, Olusola, Olufunmilayo, Omobola, and Samuel. You are all a source of joy and a team full of love. I cannot forget the little saints, my grandchildren, I love your songs and smiles, Demilade, Toni, Damilola, Tomi, and the many others on the way. I love you.

My wife, Kenny, knows me better than I know myself. She endured as I tested some of the principles I am now sharing. I cannot forget your comments and encouragement as we jointly brought up the children and taught them the principles of wealth creation. Thanks for all your love, care, and understanding. All my love for you, Kenny.

The following people who assisted me in the process of getting this book completed are appreciated. Dr Akhimien did a good job of providing motivation and correction. Your visits to the house, words of encouragement, and suggestions are deeply appreciated. You are a rare gem.

Sayo and John followed me to various places to deliver lectures on some of the topics in this book and assisted with typing and proofreading. Evangelist Joshua made it a special duty to see me comfortable and successful in building up other men. Thank you to Moji and others who helped ensure the success of this project.

The marvellous team of Westbow Press were so dedicated and committed to ensuring the success of this book. Thanks for what you did in publishing my wife's book and now my own. Your encouragement is highly appreciated. Finally, to all my friends and admirers all over the world, I thank you.

To God be the glory for the success of this work. I give Him praise, honour, and adoration.

Introduction

It is the right of everyone created by God to have wealth. There is no discrimination about getting wealthy. Age is no barrier to wealth accumulation. It is never too late, and it is never too early to start accumulating wealth. The colour of your skin or education level cannot prevent you from becoming wealthy. Your parents may not be wealthy, but this does not prevent you from becoming one of the wealthy people in your city, state, or nation. Many wealthy people are self-made. They live a lifestyle that follows the natural path of wealth and therefore become wealthy. You can also become wealthy if you desire to be wealthy and are prepared to make the necessary sacrifice for wealth accumulation.

Many people ask why they are not as wealthy as they want to be or why they are not as wealthy as their neighbour. The answer lies in your lifestyle and beliefs. Do you believe it is good to be wealthy? If you do not believe in accumulating wealth, it will be almost impossible for you to become affluent and wealthy. Those who are wealthy believe in wealth. They work towards becoming wealthy by developing new strategies to make more money and stay wealthy. If you can change your lifestyle and develop some of the characteristics of the wealthy, you will definitely see your situation changing as you consistently apply the rules of wealth.

What is Wealth?

According to the *Cambridge International Dictionary*, the word "wealth" means a large amount of money and other valuable possessions. Wealth includes money, property, investments, and other valuables. Each individual will need to determine what he or she considers to be wealth. What amount of money will you consider to be enough to think of yourself as wealthy? To some people, $1 million USD or £1 million GBP in their bank account would be adequate. Others would consider themselves wealthy if they are able to enjoy financial freedom. It is only you who can determine what you will accept as wealth.

Accumulating wealth can start at any stage in your life. You can start from where you are now. If you are determined and ready to change your lifestyle, you will accumulate wealth.

Wealth and Insolvency

Many people are acquiring properties, cars, and other valuable possessions with loans, credit cards, leases, and other forms of third-party money. Possession of these assets must be compared to total liabilities – that is, the total amount of money owed to third parties (banks, finance houses, mortgage banks, companies, individuals, and more). If your total assets are greater than your total liabilities, you have a net asset. The value of your net asset will determine the value of your wealth. If your net assets are equal to or greater than $1 million USD (or £1 million GBP or the equivalent to it), you will generally speaking be considered wealthy. If your net assets are less than $1 million, depending on the economy of your country, you may still be considered wealthy based on the circumstances in your country.

If your total assets are less than your total liabilities, you have a negative net asset, which means you are technically insolvent. This is problematic. You must take urgent steps to reverse the situation. Afterwards, you can start on a journey of wealth creation and accumulation.

Six Advantages of Wealth

1. Basic security. There should be an adequate supply of the basic necessities of life such as food and shelter.
2. Availability of purchasing power. You will be able to buy anything you want in whatever quantity you desire and at the time or place of your choice
3. The privilege of choice. Wealth will afford you the opportunity of choice as to the type of house you have and where to build it; the type of car to drive; the choice of work; and how to recreate and go on vacation.
4. Quality. You can afford the best of everything you desire. You will determine the quality you want for yourself and your family (for example, a quality education for your children).
5. Increase in wealth. You will be able to accumulate more wealth by making your money to work for you and therefore making more money.
6. Financial freedom. You will not be a debtor. You will be financially independent.

CHAPTER 1

My Story

I was born in a village where there was neither electricity nor pipe-borne water. The villagers were mainly peasant farmers and opportunities were limited.

At the age of nine, a primary school with one teacher was established in the village. All the students were in one room, which had been used as the village church before the school was established.

It was difficult for my parents to pay my school fees. Many of the children in the village could not attend the school because of the school fees. Their parents were very poor.

After two weeks the teacher, whom every villager respected because he was the most learned and informed person in the village then asked us to pay school fees. This was a small amount, but it was large for the poor peasant farmers who used hand-held farming implements. I saw poverty at its highest level at that tender age; I desired to be excluded from life in the village. This could not be achieved until I was fourteen years old.

The village school was growing, and the staff grew to three teachers. We had classes from grades one to five. The school was not approved for grade six, so all those who passed the grade five promotion examinations had to move to a bigger school in the city or a bigger village (the closest one was above five miles away).

In the latter case, it meant that there was a daily ten-mile, roundtrip trek to attend classes. My parents considered this to be too risky for a small boy like me since they were not sure whether other parents would be willing to send their children for the next class, which required the purchase of more costly books and additional school fees.

After a long deliberation, I was taken to the city to continue my education. Life was completely different, and I was overwhelmed by the cleverness of the students I met in my new school. Back in the village, because of poverty, I was always engaged in hawking food and participating in farm work, which I did not like at all, but I had to do it. I preferred hawking items from house to house within the village. I had never had the opportunity to sit down and revise any work after school hours because I had always been so tired as a result of going from house to house in order to contribute my portion of the school fees.

The students I met in the new school were very much used to revision of their work and studying together to share knowledge.

Nobody was willing to share any knowledge with me because I did not have much to offer. Also, I lived with my uncle far away and had to trek one mile from my house to the school. Though I did not have to sell any items, I was always tired after the day's work.

After failing two terminal examinations, I was faced with the option of having to repeat the class or be sent away.

My parents were borrowing money to keep me in this public school (not a private school). They hoped I was going to succeed. They did not want me to join them in the village. Hopes were high that I would pull the family out of poverty. However, I was failing my exams and had little or no clue as what I should do.

To overcome my challenges, I tried staying up late to study, but my uncle would not allow me to light the kerosene lamp. My parents were not sending money for kerosene, and I was not contributing anything in the form of learning how to sew clothes because he was a local tailor. Poverty was very visible in the house even though it was in the city. Food was rationed, and I was faced with starvation and poorer educational performance.

One day, I persuaded my mother to allow me live with my maternal grandmother. I enjoyed the privilege of being the first grandson to my maternal grandmother.

She was ready to help me become the first person to complete primary school education in the family.

She did all she could to persuade my mother to allow her to take responsibility for my life since she was in the same house with my uncle. I moved from one room to another in the same house.

I was able to study for as late as I could, and I managed to pass my examination. At the age of fifteen, I was able to complete my primary school education. The next stage was to go to the secondary school (high school). Money was the major constraint.

My father insisted that I should learn a trade and stop going to school because there was no financial capacity to start a journey of five or six years in the high school with many costly books to purchase. All entreaties from my mother and grandmother failed to persuade him.

He wanted me to be a tailor. He promised to provide me a sewing machine at the end of my apprenticeship. Poverty is not good. Every person should do all that is possible to avoid poverty. Many homes have been destroyed because of a lack of resources.

Children who are brilliant have been prevented from going to school because of poverty and a lack of knowledge on what to do to avoid poverty and create wealth.

Parents should not sentence their children to a life of limitation. There is always a way out if you are willing to try. This book is a tool to be used to change lives and improve the financial situations of families and individuals all over the world.

Back to my story, my mother vowed that she would sell her jewellery and clothes to get me started in school. Her mother, my grandmother, encouraged her. I went to school, and at the time, it was very difficult to pay the school fees.

My mother, having sold all her jewellery and clothes, sold the only cocoa farm she had. This was where money was coming in bits during the cocoa season to pay my school fees. In my final year, my grandmother also sold the only cocoa and kola nut farm she had.

The money was divided into four. My grandmother and her two daughters took three-quarters and gave it to my mother for the payment of my school fees at the high school. Her only son, who had been my guardian earlier on, refused to give her his share.

The pain at home was great after the sale of all the land; poverty increased its intensity at home. I was fully committed to my studies, knowing that so many lives had their hopes tied to my success.

After high school, there was no hope of going to the university.

I had to start working in order to send money to my mother and grandmother. My salary was small, but it was highly needed to give life to so many people in addition to maintaining myself in the city. Poverty is wicked and undesirable.

I made up my mind to get out of poverty and become a source of joy and happiness to the family. I appreciated my mother and my grandmother for what they had done to see me out of the poverty circle. I humbled myself and cut my expenses to the barest minimum.

- From my meagre salary, I started saving so I could further my studies.
- I enrolled in correspondence courses. I knew that knowledge and education would set me free from poverty.

- I later enrolled in professional banking and accounting courses.
- I refrained from going to parties and eating out. I cooked in the house and ate only breakfast in the office because of the distance from my house to the office.
- I regularly sent money to my mother and my grandmother.
- I read motivational self-help books.

After working for three years, I had saved enough money to go to a full-time technical college.

I also won a scholarship in the second year of my studies.

All the money I had paid was returned to me. That motivated me to concentrate on my professional studies, and within four years, I was qualified as a chartered certified accountant.

Life changed, but I kept doing things as though I were still living at the poverty level. I acquired experience and built up a network of friends from various backgrounds.

I learned greatly from them. I also had some mentors who guided me. The greatest breakthrough came when I met Jesus. He changed my orientation and attitude to money and success.

I started learning about God's principles for wealth, but they looked strange to me. Initially, I could not understand the principles. When I joined Full Gospel Business Men's Fellowship International, I was amazed to see young people prospering and full of joy and happiness.

I decided to surrender my life and all that I had to Jesus. I studied and put to practise the principles of God's economics, and they worked like magic in my life. I have been teaching these principles for more than two decades, and I have many testimonies about the amazing results that people have achieved using these principles.

Anyone can use them, and they will work. They will work in Africa, Asia, Europe, America, and Australia. Villagers and city dwellers alike can use the principles. In the pages of this book, I have tried to list and describe the principles.

I have also brought the ideas of great minds to your doorstep so that they can be shared with you. If you can study and apply the principles, you will be able to accelerate your success and create your own wealth. You will surely take control of your life.

As a qualified accountant, I have worked in various places, gaining experience and building networks.

In one of the companies, I was promoted several times until I became a partner. I was committed to entrepreneurship and self-sufficiency in life.

In 1980, I decided to establish a firm of chartered accountants to practice taxation, audit, and management consultancy. The firm has grown over the years; it has grown beyond the shores of my country, Nigeria. We are currently an independent member of BKR International, a leading global association of independent accounting and business advisory firms representing the expertise of more than 160 member firms with over 500 offices in over eighty countries around the world.

In addition, I am an exclusive member of International Referrals in Nigeria for accounting and insolvency.

Honour has come, and grace has come along with various opportunities. I am still studying in spite of being a fellow of many professional bodies. I went to the University to acquire more qualifications which enhanced my capacity and built me for greater achievement in life.

My mother and grandmother were the pillars upon which I leaned for my success. I appreciate the sacrifices they made for me. I am satisfied that the quality of their lives changed arising from their investment in my life which was blessed by God culminating in my eventual success.

Learn continuously, and you will enjoy your life more than those who give little attention to continuous learning.

CHAPTER 2

Why You Need to Create Wealth

Money is a very important aspect of people's lives. In my journey through life, I have seen the effects of the presence or absence of wealth in the lives of many. I have seen suffering, pain, and even untimely death resulting from poverty. Some people may ask why they need to create wealth. The following are some of the general reasons why wealth creation is important for the individual and his or her family as well as society.

2.1 Wealth Creation Gives You Financial Freedom

Financial freedom is important. Money gives you the freedom to choose what to eat, what to wear, which car to drive, the kind of school your children will attend, the kind of house and neighbourhood you will live, the people you will associate with, the kind of medical treatment you receive, and much more. In fact, money determines almost everything about your life. You are forced to send your children to just any school since that is what you can afford. You admire certain things you would have loved to have and take your eyes off those you cannot afford. Without wealth, you have no choice.

2.2 Wealth Creation Eliminates Suffering, Pain, and Lack

People are suffering. Many people cannot afford to eat good meals. Many are forced to go hungry for days. Others trek to places they would have gone in a taxi. Many others are sick and cannot go to a hospital because they do not have the money to pay the bills. There is so much suffering and unnecessary death due to lack of money. Many people do not have enough financial resources to meet their needs. With wealth, suffering and pain can be eliminated or reduced.

2.3 Wealth Reduces Crime

People suffer tremendously at the hands of poverty. They cannot meet their needs, and in the process of trying to do so, some of them go out to do anything to get the money that they need. They go into violent crime. Wealth creation can reduce crime among this category of people.

2.4 Wealth Creation Gives You Peace of Mind in Old Age

Some people become old and suddenly realize that they don't have money to look after themselves. The problem becomes worse since this is also the age that employers would ask them to retire. Others are forced to retire for health reasons. They panic. They begin to worry, leading to some of them dying prematurely. Some of them die suddenly. This could have been avoided if they had created wealth when they had the capacity to do so.

2.5 Wealth Creation Encourages Investment, Economic Growth, and National Development

When people are engaged in wealth creation, they invest in one business or the other. In the process, they employ themselves and others, thus reducing unemployment. Moreover, they and their businesses pay taxes that increase the wealth of the nation. Without wealth creation, there will be economic stagnation, poverty, and crime. It is therefore important to create wealth for the general growth of the economy.

2.6 Wealth Creation Enables You to Leave Inheritance for Your Loved Ones

Your spouse and children should not be left uncared for when you depart from this earth. Your wealth will be available to meet their needs, especially if you die suddenly. It is necessary for you to leave legacy for your children.

2.7 The Wealth You Create Will Ameliorate the Suffering of Others

If used well, your wealth will contribute to resources needed by charity and faith-based organizations to care for the needs of humanity.

2.8 Wrong Belief about Wealth

- ❖ High income is wealth. This is not true. There is a difference between income and wealth. You can earn a very high income, but if you spend all of it, you will not be wealthy. Those who spend all their income are simply living high. They cannot accumulate wealth. It is what you accumulate that makes you wealthy, not what you spend on living.
- ❖ You will become wealthy through luck. This is not true. It is rare that people become wealthy through luck. Wealth comes more often through self-discipline, hard work, frugality, perseverance, planning, and commitment.
- ❖ I will become wealthy when I win the lottery or receive a windfall. This happens to very few people. It is very rare to see people who became rich and sustain the wealth in this manner. Most people who become wealthy did so over time. Wealth is accumulated slowly and steadily and by living a lifestyle that is conducive to wealth accumulation.

- ❖ Wealthy people spend lavishly and drive expensive cars. When I become a millionaire, I will live in an expensive and exclusive neighbourhood. I will drive the latest luxury car. With these type of beliefs, it will be difficult – if not impossible – to become wealthy. Most wealthy people do not crave luxury.

CHAPTER 3

What Hinders Wealth Creation?

In this chapter, we shall examine the challenges to wealth creation. We will answer several questions. What are the challenges to wealth creation? Why is it that people cannot create wealth? Why is it difficult for people to create wealth? Why is it that people are not creating wealth despite the fact that they desire good things of life?

3.1 Failure to Recognize Wealth-Creation Ideas and Opportunities

The main reason that has been identified is the problem of how to recognize opportunities and wealth-creation ideas. People often don't recognize opportunities because opportunities don't come shouting that they are opportunities. They often come disguised as problems or challenges. They must be carefully sought out and identified by those who are ready or willing to search for them. People find it difficult to recognize an opportunity when it comes.

An example is when there is a new law in an area. Whenever there is a change in law or any form of change at all, this becomes opportunity for people to examine and see what is in it for them. What is in this new thing for you that you can learn or that you already know that can now get other people to come to you for a solution? People have to recognize when an opportunity comes their way. Opportunities associated with change are numerous and will always be available for those who look out for them whenever there is a change.

3.2 Inability to Generate Wealth-Creating Ideas

There are ideas that will not create wealth. For example, some may not generate more income than expenditure. If you want to create wealth, the income must be more than what you will have to expend before you generate the income. In other words, your idea must be able to make a net income after you have deducted all the expenses. If you are to run a business, the income from the business must be more than the total expenses after providing for your own remuneration and that of anyone else who may be working with you in the business.

Charity is charity, and business is business. When you do charity, you are not expected to make profit from it. You have to look for donors to support the venture. However, donors get weary after a while and expect you to do a self-sufficient programme after some time. They may help you to start it, but after a time, they will expect you to be self-financing. So even if you are going into charity, you cannot continue to depend on donors. You must have a way to make it self-sufficient after a while.

3.3 Improper Management of Resources

The next one is the challenge of improper management of resources. Some people have opportunities and resources at their disposal but are not able to make use of them. Some of these resources are briefly discussed below.

Time

The number-one resource people waste is time. Life is in stages. One's life can be divided into four phases: from year zero to eighteen; from eighteen to forty, from forty to sixty, and sixty and above. There are things you are supposed to do from zero to eighteen. For example, you are expected to be learning values, going to school, and determining what profession you want to go into. From ages 18 to 40 you are expected to finish schooling, take up a job and start planning your future. Once any of this time is wasted, it is difficult – if not impossible – to recover it. Some people spend their time on frivolities instead of planning and investing; they are consequently forced to continue to struggle for a means of livelihood at the time they ought to be resting.

For example, some people suddenly realize by the time they are fifty that they don't have a house. If they are asked to leave work, they have nowhere to go. Sadly, too, by the time they are fifty, some people have health issues. Thus, they will be unable to continue to do what they used to do. Since there are younger people with agility and youthful vigour, they are laid off by their employers whose primary interest is the growth of their businesses. Finding a new job at age fifty is difficult. Wasted time is a major challenge to wealth creation. It is important for everyone to invest when one has the time to do so. That is at the early stage of life. There are those who started late and achieved tremendous success. That is not the norm – it is exceptional.

Wasted Inherited Assets

Some people waste their assets, including property or buildings. For example, there are people whose parents died, leaving them with a big house. They move into the house. Since they lack the means to effectively maintain it, the house starts deteriorating. This is a case of wasting assets. The one thing a person could do is to ask a professional for advice or an architect to remodel the place (for example, create apartments for him and for rent). The money from the rent can then be used to maintain his own apartment and himself. There may even be some money left to save or invest.

Wasted Salaries and Other Incomes

Another resource that people often waste is salaries and other incomes. For example, consider a man who initially earns $100,000 and has an increase to $150,000. Instead of planning how he would save some of the money, he spends it on expensive cars and other unnecessary luxuries.

In addition, he would fail to realize that regardless of what he is being paid, the job is only an opportunity for him to learn. He is not supposed to be permanently there. A job ought to be seen as a learning period and a period to acquire capital to start his own business, something he can fall back on at retirement. Unfortunately, that is not the case, and such people end up wasting their incomes. They live big, buying big cars that consume too much of their resources.

3.4 Lack of Wealth-Creation Strategies

Some people cannot create wealth because they lack wealth-creation strategies. To create wealth, you need an appropriate strategy. Many let their environmental elements and forces control them. They are reactive. To create wealth, you must think proactively. You must make things happen and not watch things happen. You have to create your world. When you don't have a strategy, you are supposed to ask others.

3.5 Failure to Develop Oneself

Another challenge to wealth creation is people's failure to develop themselves. Everything around us is changing. To remain relevant, one must develop oneself. There are courses all over the place. There are universities that encourage part-time education; there are even short courses that one can attend and develop oneself at technical colleges and polytechnics. Professional institutions are also available for continuous development. Technology has made it possible to study online. You can be exposed to fresh ideas and knowledge. After that, you are better equipped to do what you intend to do.

3.6 Unorganized Efforts

- Planning. Planning is essential for success in life. Imagine how difficult it will be to build a mansion without a building plan. Apart from wasting of materials, time will also be wasted. Men and women who succeed in life do not get there haphazardly. Rather, they pursue a set action plan to attain a desired goal.

Wealth creation is a major undertaking that should be of great importance to you and your family. To ensure success, you must create plans. If your first plan does not work successfully, please replace it with a new plan. If the new plan also fails to work, do not hesitate to replace it with another plan. Continue until you find a plan that works. People fail because of a lack of persistence. Planning takes time and effort. You must persist until you are able to create a plan that will suit your purpose.

Planning involves setting out, in clear terms, things to do and how to do them in order to achieve the expected result. Planning is crucial. It involves choosing causes of action to achieve an objective. It concerns the future, and it reduces waste. Limited resources available are used efficiently.

If you are interested in moving from one higher ground to another and to stand out among your equals, you must master the act of regular planning.

- Lack of information. Wealth creation requires gathering of vital and relevant information. Information brings transformation. People become uninformed when they lack information. You

must access information and data. You must learn how to gather information.
- Laziness. No lazy man or a woman has a future. You will never find an achiever who is not a successful hard worker. If you go through the story of successful people in the world, you will find out that no one ever rose to the top who was not a proven hard worker. Every man of height and dignity in the world today is a notable hard worker. It is impossible to see success without hard working.

Poor control. It is one thing to be successful. It is another thing to remain successful. Success is a journey; it is not a destination in itself. Anybody may get to the top, but not everybody can remain at the top. It is important to be disciplined. Some people don't have money today because they were not disciplined enough to control their spending. They allowed poor control to rob them of a future that is sure of comfort, happiness, and joy.

Everyone should take a lesson from ants, especially those who are lazy. The ants are small insects that have no prince, governor, or ruler to command and supervise them to work. However, they work very hard throughout the summer gathering the food they will eat in the winter. Unfortunately, some people keep on sleeping, procrastinating, and wasting time instead of doing their work and preparing for the challenges of life.

If you do not make a change by learning from the ant, before you know it, poverty will pounce on you like a bandit, scarcity will attack you like an armed robber.

"Go to the ants ye sluggard; consider her ways and be wise. Which having no guide, overseer or ruler provideth her meat in summer; and gathereth her food in the harvest.

How long will thou sleep, O sluggard? Yet a little sleep, a little slumber a little folding of the hands to sleep. So shall thy poverty come as one that travelleth and thy want as an armed man." (Proverbs 6: 6–11, KJV).

CHAPTER 4

You Need a Vision: Your Bridge to a Successful Future

Vision is essential for success in anything you desire. A man or woman with vision will achieve so much when compared to another with the same ability and opportunities but who lacks vision. If you have a vision, you will have a direction. Most successful people are people of vision.

We should know that vision is crucial to our achieving the purpose of God, but many people do not understand the concept of vision. Without defined vision, people wander about, achieving little or nothing in life.

Such people are unable to maximize their potential. The visionless hardly know how to channel their resources and energy. They find it difficult to accomplish great achievements. It is important to know that vision is a crucial resource for an outstanding life of success and wealth creation.

4.1 What is Vision?

According to George Barna in his book, *The Power of Vision*, "Vision is a mental picture held in your mind of some preferred future experience and developments." Vision is like a bridge that links you from your present position to a better and preferred future. As you pass through life, you are crossing the bridge to the brighter future contained within your vision. It involves a change from the present situation to something better. No matter the position you find yourself in now, you deserve a better future. Both the rich and the poor need a better future. Vision is for everyone, and vision involves change. Your future should be better than your present.

In your mind's eye, you will hold that image of a better future where you will be a rich and wealthy person. You are the only one having that picture in your mind. No one else can see it until you paint that picture and make it a reality.

The vision is unique to you. You have to rely on God to make the picture a reality in your life, as you tread the path of life's journey. All your past achievements and failures must be set aside as you focus your attention on the preferred future. It is your future, a better, richer, and surer future. You have to make that picture of a better future real to you and cherish it.

4.2 Importance of a Vision

Vision keeps you focused. "Where there is no vision the people perish, but he that keepeth the law Happy is he" (Proverbs 29: 18, KJV). One important thing about vision is that it will enable you to know the direction you are going in life. You will not be going about in circles. Your efforts and resources will not be wasted.

- Vision is crucial for success. A written vision serves as a compass. A ship cannot do without a compass because it guides it on the high sea. You need a written vision, which is like a compass or a map to aid you on your journey in life. This includes creation and accumulation of wealth.
- Vision will assist you within your ability and talents. Some people try to become something different from what God has purposed

for them. If you work with God in receiving your vision, it will confirm the gifts or ability in you and the things you desire to do.
- Vision will see you through difficult times. In times of crisis, you will refer to your vision. It may be tough, but you will surely be convinced of success as you stand firm, refusing to deviate from your vision. Most people who survive in times of crisis are people with a clearly defined vision.
- Your vision will give you hope. If you can determine your God-given vision, you will develop confidence and hope. It may be difficult, but take steps to work with God in determining your vision. Hold fast to it, and you will rejoice in the end. Your vision will enable you to see the possibility of achieving something you previously thought to be impossible.
- Vision gives a defined destination. Just as an airline ticket carries a defined destination, your vision gives you a destination. You will know your performance as you proceed to the destination.
- Vision will bring change into your life. Vision usually brings change. With vision, you cannot permanently be at a dead end. A change will definitely occur, and it is a change for the better future. This change will give you happiness and joy.
- Vision makes your life unique. Vision is personal. It will make you innovative and creative. Vision is your unique bridge to cross from the present to a better future. No other person has the same vision as you. The decision is yours. The picture is in your mind. You have to paint it and make it a reality.
- Vision protects you against waste of life. Vision ensures that you do not waste your resources, talents, abilities, and creativity. Your vision will stand as your defence against negative wasters.

4.3 Document Your Vision

It is essential that you write down the vision. If you write down the vision, it will clearly indicate the person you would be and what you will achieve in life. It will become your compass as you navigate through the ocean of life. A written vision is like a map to guide in finding your way in life as you create wealth and maximize your talents.

"And the Lord answered me, and said, Write the vision, and make it plain upon tables, that he may run that readeth it." (Habakkuk 2:2, KJV)

You have to write down your vision and read it clearly and quickly as you pass through life.

4.4 Vision Killers

There are many reasons why people do not accomplish their God-given vision. The vision is killed at one stage of the process, and, if not renewed, the person becomes visionless. Drifting will set in. You should be careful to avoid a premature death of your vision. We shall now look into some of the vision killers.

4.4.1 Fear

Fear is a major vision killer. Such fear can be divided into four categories: fear of change, fear of the unknown, fear of failure, and fear of destruction.

4.4.2 Fear of Change

People are used to a particular way of doing things and a particular way of life, and they are unwilling to change. They are afraid to break out of their comfort zone, doing a new thing in areas where they have no record of success. Vision is about the future; it involves change. If you are afraid of change, your vision will easily die unaccomplished.

4.4.3 Fear of the Unknown

Fear grips people whenever they are confronted with the unknown. They become uncomfortable because they are not sure of the outcome of the unknown. Their confidence level becomes low. This type of fear will weaken your vision and eventually wipe out your vision if you allow it.

4.4.5 Fear of Failure

Because they have failed in the past, some people are reluctant to take another step into the unknown. They prefer to operate at a level where they can confidently point to a track record of success. You have to forget the past and face the future. Your failures should not hinder your progress. Do not be afraid to embrace your God-given vision. Do not allow fear to kill your vision. Some people may not have failed in the past, but they fear failure regardless. Their pride is easily wounded when they record any failure. Failure is a challenge for a better performance. Failure is an experience on how not to do something. If you want success, you should not be scared of failure. Those who operate only under conditions they consider safe are restricting themselves. The fear of failure will cause you to miss your only opportunity. Remember that vision replaces fear with determination, energy, and hope. The Bible is full of encouragement that will enable you to overcome fear.

Jeremiah 29: 11 (KJV) says, "For I know the thoughts I have towards you. They are thoughts of good and not of evil to give you an expected end."

Joshua 1: 9 (KJV) says, "Have I not commanded thee? Be strong and be of good courage: Be not afraid, neither be thou dismayed: for the Lord thy God is with thee withersoever thou goest."

If you leave God out of your vision for life, you will have fear. 2 Timothy 1: 7 (KJV) says, "For God has not given us the spirit of fear; but of power, and of love and of sound mind."

Fear has nothing to do with you if you believe the promises of God. If you work with God in the process of recalling your vision, you will not be entertaining fear.

4.4.6 Fear of Destruction

People are afraid of destruction. Most people do not want to die. If a vision affects movement to a new location – or doing a new type of business – the fear of safety for their lives in the new location may grip them. Because they have not lived in the new location before and have no relations or friends who can assure them of their safety, they will be reluctant to change.

"After these things the words of God the Lord came unto Abram in a vision. Saying Fear not, Abram; I am thy shield and thy exceeding great reward." (Genesis 15: 1, KJV)

4.4.7 Short-Term Thinking

Many people are preoccupied with immediate gains. In the shortest term, they want gains. Such people are not concerned with the future. They are myopic. People who pursue immediate gains are robbing themselves of a better future. Vision involves the future. It is long term in nature. If you think in the short term, you will kill God's vision for your life. Your accomplishment will be small and short-lived.

4.4.8 Complacency

Many people have had their vision killed by complacency. They believe that regardless of what they do, God is unable to bless their efforts. However, God is interested in what we do. He will bless our efforts if they are in line with His plans for us. Vision requires energy and vigour. You should apply yourself and your energy to the vision that God has given to you. Give your vision all that you have and ensure that you maintain a cordial relationship with God.

4.4.9 Fatigue

Vision calls for energy and effort. Wealth accumulation requires planning, energy, and effort. Allow for rest as you go along with your vision for wealth creation. You cannot receive direction for your vision when you are tired and exhausted. You must rest and work on your vision, spending quality time when you are fresh and full of energy for that vision to be realized.

4.4.10 People

Do not allow people to kill your vision. Some people are visionless, and they specialize in discouraging others. No matter what you do, they will not see the good to be accomplished. Such people are like Sanballat and Tobias in the fourth chapter of the book of Nehemiah. They ridiculed Nehemiah and the Israelites who were building the wall in Jerusalem. They did everything to discourage them. Nehemiah did not allow himself to be discouraged. Do not allow people like Sanballat and Tobias to kill your vision. Do not allow yourself to be discouraged by the visionless people. Move away from vision killers and create wealth.

4.4.11 Sin

The remuneration for sin is both spiritual and physical death. If you sin, you will be cast off from God. As soon as you sin, you have fallen short of the glory of God. The sinful nature will control. In these conditions, you cannot receive a vision or direction for a vision from God. The way forward is to confess your sins. God is faithful and just, and He will forgive you of your sins and purify you from all unrighteousness. Turn away from those sins, and build a new relationship with God. He is waiting for you. Do not delay. Seek for God, and He will reward you.

4.4.12 Lack of Faith

A lack of faith will constantly bring fear to your mind. You will not be able to focus. A lack of faith will result in a lack of vision. Have faith in God, trust in Him, and thank Him. He will give you what you want, including your vision and the achievement of your goals.

"And Jesus answering saith unto them. Have Faith in God." (Mark 11: 22, KJV).

"Trust in the Lord with All thine heart and lean not unto thy own understanding." (Proverbs 3: 5, KJV)

4.4.13 Demonic Forces

In some cases, demonic forces kill vision. They operate in the form of witchcraft or occultism. The demonic forces monitor the life of the person of their target and block his progress. They could cause him to lose focus or paralyze his efforts to succeed. When such things happen, he will abandon his vision and lose direction. Prayer will set you free so that you should accomplish God's purposes for your life.

4.4.14 Bad Habits and Indiscipline

These two spell doom for any vision or endeavours, whether secular or spiritual. Any form of training of the mind and character to produce self-control and habits of obedience is crucial for the accomplishment of any vision including creation of wealth.

Obedience and self-denial are key to the attainment of our visions. We must learn to submit ourselves to training or discipline before we can make any headway in the race of life. All bad habits must be changed. Discipline must be embraced to ensure success of your vision and achievement of the goal of creating and accumulating wealth.

4.4.15 Envy and Jealousy

Envy is a feeling of disappointment and resentment at another's better fortune. When we show unhappiness because of the better fortune of others, jealousy becomes synonymous with envy. When one is eaten up with envy, the necessary drive for attainment of any vision becomes completely eroded. Team spirit is broken up, and the resultant disunity depletes our store of energy. The future is adversely affected. Run away from envy. Don't be jealous about the success of others.

4.4.16 Lack of Forgiveness

A lack of forgiveness inhibits growth and blocks every true quest for a God-given vision. Your mind will become deceased, and the body generally becomes weak when we harbour enmity or any form of malice against our fellow men.

You can neither think nor pray properly when you fail to forgive your neighbour or yourself. It is an outright rejection of the will of God and often causes the body to malfunction, leading to various terminal diseases and making it impossible for any spiritual communion to take place. You need to walk out of every self-imposed captivity by setting free as many as are being held captive in your mind; that way, you can receive direction from God. Make it easy for you to forgive those who have offended or will offend you in the future. Your vision and your goals should not be truncated through your failure to forgive those who offend you.

Ultimately, vision will give you hope and confidence, and you will find it easy and enjoyable to create and accumulate wealth.

CHAPTER 5

Establish Goals

You need to sit down and write down the things you want to achieve in life. You will have to divide them into short-, medium-, and long-terms goals.

Short-term goals are the goals you want to achieve within the next one to two years.

Medium-term goals range from two to five years. Long-term goals are to be achieved within the next five to ten years or more. The goals should be prioritized. They should be time-bound, measurable, specific, realistic, and achievable.

It is important that you write down the goals and refer to them frequently. As you do so, you are pouring energy into the goals. Their realization will be easier than you can imagine. Concentrating on your goals is very important if you want success. Stay on track and refuse to deviate from your goals regardless of the daily pressures and challenges of life. The more you stay on your goals, the more circumstances will submit themselves to your will. This will permit you to achieve your goals faster. It will also be an additional advantage for goal achievement if you can make use of visualization. If you can visualize achieving those goals, you will discover that your aims will be accomplished. It is important that your vision is clear, specific, and written down. Your mind will be able to focus on clear and frequently visualized goals, thereby ensuring early realization of your goals.

The powerful tool of goal setting can be used daily, weekly, monthly, and annually as well as for periodic times in the course of your life for the purpose of achieving your aims (including the accumulation of wealth).

5.1 Aim High

Desire is the most important requirement in the process of wealth accumulation. It is more important than special ability or academic intelligence. If you have a strong desire to be wealthy, and you combine it with good planning and extra effort, you will achieve unprecedented level of wealth creation in your life. Extraordinary financial achievement calls for a strong desire, serious planning, and extra efforts. You will have an edge over your peers if you can start now by aiming high for a better future. There is no limit to how much wealth you can accumulate. There is no limit to your level of achievement – it depends on you. You are the one who can limit yourself. Aim high and plan for success in your life. In all your plans, include financial freedom. This will ensure that you are free from debts and pressures as you accumulate and retain wealth.

5.2 Building Your Wealth

It is essential that you set a wealth plan. Many people are not able to set up a plan because of the effort required to do so. They procrastinate, and they may not do any planning for their future. Some people make a will. This is a plan for death. They plan for the distribution of their assets and settlement of any liabilities at the time of their death. Why can't you prepare a plan for living? It is a wealth plan that will be an instrument to guide your life to financial freedom and ensure achievement of your dreams. You need a plan for wealth accumulation. It is never too late or too early to start on your journey to that dream land of the wealth where only a few are successful. Please start today. Establish your wealth plan. You will be able to know clearly where you want to go. You can get there quickly. The power of goal setting will be available for you to achieve extraordinary results.

5.3 The Wealth Plan

Your vision is the bridge between where you are now and the better future you desire. You will need to prepare a plan that will lead you to the preferred and better future with financial freedom. There are six stages in the plan.

1. Determine where you are now.
2. Establish where you want to be.
3. Choose the strategies for getting to your destination.
4. Change your lifestyle.
5. Protect your wealth and get wealthier.
6. Review your wealth plan periodically.

5.4 Where Are You Now?

It is important to know your financial position. That is the state of your affairs at a particular date. What are your assets? What are your liabilities (the amount you owe to people)? Let us start with your assets.

Assets

1. Landed property (a) Your home (if owned by you)
   (b) Land (developed or underdeveloped)
   (c) Any other building owned by you

   State the realistic current value. Also state any mortgage or loans outstanding on the property listed.

2. Automobiles (a) Realistic value of any automobile owned by you
   (b) The value of any outstanding loans on the automobiles
3. Life assurance (a) The surrender value of any assurance policies you hold
4. Pension (a) The current value of your pension fund
5. Valuables (a) The value of the jewellery, gold, diamonds, and the like you possess
6. Savings
   (a) Cash deposits and fixed deposits
   (b) Accrued interest currency
   (c) Building society deposits
7. Investments (a) Share certificates at market value
   (b) Unit trusts at market value
   (c) Bonds at market value
   (d) Other investments at market value
8. Household goods

Please note that the valuations should be realistic. Any overvaluation is not to your advantage. Valuation by external persons, for example, estate agents is preferred.

Household goods should be valued conservatively to arrive at a realistic figure. The table below will represent an illustration of the value of your assets at realistic values.

Table 1 Assets

	$
1. Landed property: Home	150,000
Underdeveloped land	30,000
2. Automobiles: Car	3,000
Truck	5,000
3. Life insurance (surrender value)	11,000
4. Pension	40,000
5. Valuables: Jewellery	10,000
Gold bar	15,000
6. Savings: Cash deposits	15,000

Fixed Deposit	20,000
7. Investments: Shares	25,000
Bonds	15,000
8. Household goods: Furniture	2,000
Air conditioners	5,000
Others	<u>2,000</u>
Total	**348,000**
	=========

Liabilities

List all the money that you owe to determine the total of what you are to pay to third parties.

- Credit card debts: List all the cards and the amount outstanding on each card.
- Store debts: List all the store cards and the amount outstanding on each card.
- Loans: Bank loans and bank overdrafts
- Other Loans: List the amount of loans outstanding from financial institutions or nonfinancial institutions. Do not leave out any loan or indebtedness, no matter how small or large it may be. Whatever may be the source of the loan, make sure it is listed. It is the outstanding amount that you will list out. The total of them is your total liability.
- Lease agreements: List the amount outstanding on each lease.
- Hire purchase agreements: List the monthly payments multiplied by the number of months outstanding.

HOW TO CREATE WEALTH AND AVOID POVERTY

Table 2 below shows example of how your liability may be. All the items may not relate to you. Take those that relate to you and add them together to get the total value of your liabilities.

Table 2 Liabilities	$
1. Credit card: Standard Chartered Bank	5,000
Barclays Bank	3,000
2. Marks & Spencer card	3,500
3. Bank overdraft: Maxim Bank	1,500
4. Outstanding lease on car	6,000
5. Bank loans: Guarantee Trust Bank	2,000
First International Bank	3,000
6. Other loans: Cooperative Society	1,500
Cousin Joy	2,000
Total	**27,500**

The next thing to do is to compare your total liabilities with your assets. The difference is your net worth, which is the total of assets minus the total of your liabilities. If the liabilities are more than the total assets, it shows that you will need to find a way to start repayment of your debts. You will be starting in the negative, and you must do something about it quickly (for example, increasing your income). This will give you the chance to have some funds to invest.

If your assets are more than your liabilities, you can start with your plan for investment as part of the process for building up your wealth. Table 3 is an illustration of how to determine your net worth.

Table 3 **Net worth**	$
Total assets (as per Table 1)	348,000
Less total liabilities (as per Table 2)	27,500
Total	**320,500**

Some people consider the process of ascertaining where they are financially to be tedious and time-consuming. However, if you do not know where you are, it will be difficult to plan for you to leave where you are presently and go to where you want to be financially. Determine your net worth, and you will know what you are worth now. The bigger your net worth, the wealthier you become. You need to improve your net worth from time to time.

Where do you want to be? It is necessary for you to establish where you want to be financially. Set the goals for your wealth accumulation. Goals will energize you.

Continue to Set Goals

Goals will give you energy and make you to be focused. Wealthy people are focused people. They set goals and work assiduously towards achieving the goals. As one goal is achieved, they set another one. You too can develop the habit of setting goals. It is good to have your mind fixed on what you want to achieve by putting it down in the form of a goal to be pursued with all your strength. You will also want to request assistance from God.

Your goals could be short-term and long-term.

Short-Term Goals

- I will pay all my credit card debts by 31 December.
- I will move into my own rented apartment by 31 December.
- I will leave my job and start my own small business by 31 January.

Do not list too many goals. Aim for important goals that will align with your vision. Let the goals be such that it will excite you to achieve them.

Long-Term Goals

- I will build (purchase) my own house by 30 June, 20XX.

- I will obtain a second passport from another country by 31 December, 20XX. Thereby becoming a dual citizen.
- I will become a millionaire by 31 August, 20XX, when I will be XX years old.
- I will expand my business to cover five different countries.
- I will obtain a university diploma in business administration by 20xx.

Your long-term goals are yours. Make sure you have the reason to desire these goals and that they are yours, not goals to please or excite your spouse or parents. If they are yours, make sure you have reasons for setting those goals. If you have genuine reasons, you will take every step to achieve them. You will be motivated to face any situation on your way to achieving the goals. It will be easier if you make the goals known to God. God knows more than you do. He will direct your paths if you commit your ways and goals to Him. Another thing you need to know is that you should be clear in your mind about each goal. Describe the goal in detail, and write it down. Note a time by which you intend to achieve the goal. This will enable you to measure your performance as you live your life.

Action. You have to take actions towards achieving your goal. Every day, you should move forward. Do things that will take you nearer to the goal.

Review and Measurement. You need to regularly review and measure your performance. On a daily, weekly, and monthly basis, take steps to measure how far you have moved on your journey to creating wealth. If you discover that you are slow, take steps to increase your actions, work harder, or change your strategy. Monitoring and evaluating will ensure that you achieve your goals.

CHAPTER 6

Hints on Lifestyles that Will Enhance Accumulation of Wealth

Many people are looking for the magic formular that will help them to accumulate wealth. They want it short and simple. I can assure you there are no such formulars. You can ask those who are rich how they got there. You will be surprised nobody will be able to give an assured formular for wealth accumulation.

However, you will be informed by those who have passed through the journey of wealth accumulation that lifestyle is important if you want to accumulate wealth and avoid poverty.

In this section, some hints and lifestyles which have improved financial freedom and wealth accumulation for me are shared to assist you.

As you go along the journey of wealth accumulation you will discover other lifestyes that will assist you. They are guides to stimulate you for change in lifestyle if you desire to succeed in your set goals of wealth accumulation.

They are:

1. Live well beneath your means.

2. If you earn money and spend it all, you cannot accumulate wealth. It is important that you spend less than your income. The balance and its interest should be saved so your money can work for you.
3. Choose the right occupation to promote wealth accumulation

   What is your occupation? Can it generate enough income to provide for your needs and leave something extra to save? Change your occupation if necessary. Continuous development is essential for wealth creation and accumulation.

4. Plan your time and efficiently allocate your available time, energy, and resources.

   Always renew your energy by having short breaks. Use your time wisely and plan your activities and operations accordingly.

5. Build up skills as well as your efficiency in the recognition and targeting of opportunities.

   Your skills must be targeted, not mere acquisition of certificate. Your skills must add value that people are willing to pay for. You must be efficient. Target opportunity, and develop relevant skills.

6. Remember that it is more important to have financial freedom than to display high levels of social status.

   Living high will not create wealth. Remember that the high income you have today will not continue indefinitely

7. Train your children and motivate them to grow to be self-sufficient economically.
8. Imbibe the quality of a compulsive saver who saves all of the time, regardless of income size.

   Saving is a habit that requires discipline. Develop the habit and discipline yourself to save regularly.

9. Develop skills for regular and efficient investment of resources.

    Whatever you have saved must be invested wisely to create wealth. Learn about investment. Do not simply hand over your hard-earned money to somebody to invest for you. Be involved and acquire a basic understanding of investment

10. Be diligent in your business and workplace.

    If you are diligent, nothing will hinder your progress. Do not be careless with your business. Take responsibility and commit yourself to excellence. You will be rewarded handsomely.

11. Plan and be self-disciplined

    Planning is very essential for your success in life, especially in creating wealth. Planning will make you focused. You will have a target to work towards. Put it in mind to be a regular planner, and always make a revision of your plan as a way of determining whether you have met your goals.

12. Persevere and always go through the extra mile.

    Persistence is a major key to success in wealth creation. Don't give up, and don't be intimidated by challenges. Arise and move up again.

13. Do not provide fish for your adult children. Rather, teach them how to fish. Build up their capacity to provide for themselves.
14. Do not allow yourself to be carried away by success. Maintain your focus, and demonstrate humility and the fear of God
15. Value relationships (with your spouse, your business partners, and your maker).

    You must not operate in isolation. You need your spouse and others to cooperate with you to ensure success. More importantly, you need your maker to give you the supernatural power to create and accumulate wealth.

16. When there is distress, call on God, listen to His instruction, and obey and carry the instruction out. Receive the solution by faith, and tell the story when your success comes.

CHAPTER 7

Strategies for Wealth Creation

7.0 Introduction

For everything that is successful, there is always a strategy. There are strategies for wealth creation. In this chapter, we shall discuss these strategies. A strategy is a series of action plans designed to achieve a particular objective or set of objectives. Your wealth-creation strategies will be actions you will take to enable you achieve the goals of wealth creation and accumulation. The strategies will include the followings:

7.1 Persistence

You must never give up even when it appears you are not going to achieve your goal. Even if you fail, don't give up. With persistence, you will succeed. If you persist and don't give up, you will achieve your goal of creating wealth. Those who give up don't have a story to tell.

You must not surrender to the challenges of life. The power to hang it there is often what separates between those who turn out to be victors and those who become helpless victims.

To persist means to carry on, to go on, or to hang on until you are through. It means to refuse to give up or quit.

The Persistent Woman

This is a story I read all the time, and I love it. It is the story of a woman who had a problem with someone. The woman asked a judge to help her with the person who had wronged her. But not feeling obliged to do so, the judge ignored the woman. The judge's refusal did not deter her, and the woman pestered the judge day and night. After some time, the judge said, "Although I don't fear God and I don't fear anybody, if I don't help this woman, she would kill me with her worry. Let me do this thing for her so that she can go. I will be relieved of her pestering." At that, he attended to her. Her persistence paid off.

7.2 Restrategize if Necessary

Although you need to persist, common sense sometimes dictates the need to re-examine your strategy in light of changing circumstances. If it becomes obvious that the old strategy won't achieve your aim, you need to adopt a new strategy. For example, if you want to pass through a mountain, and you suddenly get there to meet a big rock, one strategy is to pass through it by climbing over the rock. If you cannot climb the rock, you may change your strategy by drilling a hole though the rock. Likewise, you may need to go around the rock to get to the other side. If possible, you can get something or someone that would lift you up and put you on the other side. You can't create wealth if you give up.

7.3 Continuous Development

One thing that is constant in life is change. Knowledge keeps you going ahead in life. If you must create wealth, you must continuously acquire knowledge. Get knowledge from schools and books. Attend short courses, workshops, and seminars. The Internet is also a great reservoir of knowledge. Look for information only from reputable sources.

If possible, acquire additional degrees that will enhance your performance at work. On the job, learning is very important. Know your job, and be an expert in it. Continually improve your knowledge and skills.

7.4 Effective Time Management

Those who want to create wealth manage their time effectively. Time is your life, and it must be properly utilized. Of all the resources available to man, time is the only one that cannot be reclaimed, so it is very important to spend it well. Time must be spent on productive ventures. Some people spend time on things that will not add value to them or enhance their chances of succeeding in life. There are many books on time management. Learn how others have organized their lives by planning and effective utilization of timing. Creation and accumulation of wealth demands effective utilization of timing

7.5 Have Your Own Wealth-Creation Plan

Every human being should have a wealth-creation plan. You must have one, and you must continue to monitor your wealth-creation plan. Your wealth-creation plan is very important. It is all about your life, and it is all about your future. Therefore, you must make sure that it is in order at all times. If anything changes, you must make corrections so that you can achieve your plan. You must work the plan. Sometimes, you will need other people to help you. You must employ those people and if you need to pay those people to make your plan come through, then pay them. You will see that your plan will be achieved.

7.6 Continuously Renew Your Life (Physical Exercise)

To continue to be effective, you also have to renew yourself. You must physically renew your life through bodily exercise. You must eat good food so that your body continues to get what it needs to function properly. You also need rest to prevent unnecessary breakdowns. It is important. Regular exercise is important for you to keep fit to work and create wealth.

7.7 Build Relationships

No man is an island. In your journey to creating wealth, you need other people. You must work with people, and you need to build relationships. You need a network of people. To build relationships, you must help people actualize their dreams. In turn, they will help you realize your goals.

You will never become your best all by yourself. Success is a result of the accumulation of great relationships. If you place value on people, they will add value to your life. The more help you get from people, the further you will go in life. Marital relationship is useful for wealth creation. If you are unmarried, it will be helpful to plan to get married. If you are married, keep the relationship healthy, caring, and loving. It is very rewarding to have a spouse who believes in you and your vision. Keep your loved ones happy and honoured. Bless your spouse and your children with good words.

7.8 Renew Yourself Mentally

To create wealth, you need to continuously renew your brain by reading. When the brain is used, it is sharpened. When it is not used, it deteriorates. That is when you find out that you are beginning to lose memory. Always try to learn something new (perhaps a new language) or do something that tasks your brain, so that your brain gets sharper.

Make every effort to make yourself more effective in whatever you are doing. You must keep learning all your life. Read something, even if it is only ten or fifteen minutes daily. You will be amazed at amount of knowledge you will accumulate. Your brain is like a computer – it has a very large storage capacity. Those things that you are learning are stored for your future use.

Another way to develop yourself is through listening to teachings on various topics on tapes, CDs and webcasts. You can also participate in quiz competitions or debates.

Related Story

I didn't know how to use the computer until I was fifty years old. I had bought one for my children which they were using.. When I asked them to teach me how to use it, they would laugh at me and didn't take me seriously. Realising that they would not teach me to use it, I decided that I was going to England to learn to use computers, and I did. In England, I registered for a two-week computer course in a school where I was taught along side people of my children's age. I didn't care when they were laughing because they were not my children, they were my teachers, and I was their student. I humbled myself to learn from them. In the end, I acquired the computer literacy I needed.

Although I was then a computer literate, I still didn't know how to use the Internet. I knew I needed this additional knowledge. I decided that I would go back to the computer school in England. So I went and learned about the online world. From that time on, I didn't allow my knowledge to deteriorate. Whenever my children were online at home, I joined them and learned with them. We are in the information age. You must be part of it – don't be left behind.

7.9 Have a Budget and Save Money

A budget is mandatory for wealth creation. A budget is simply a plan containing your income and planned expenditures. You must have not only a budget, but you also must continually monitor your budget. I will illustrate the importance of budgeting with the following story.

John's Story

There were four men in a village working in the same company. They had worked for that company for a very long time. After a while, the head of the village found out that one of them, Mr John, was prospering while the others were not. At that time, John had four houses in the village. Anytime the village wanted to do anything developmental, he would always contribute more than the other three. So the village decided that it was going to honour him on a particular day. Preparations were made, and people were called to come. The village informed John that he was going to tell the story of how he was able to have four houses and lives more comfortably than all his colleagues.

When the time came for him to speak, he thanked the village leaders and said that while he was aware that women were not normally allowed to speak on such matters, he wanted his wife to be allowed to speak. The matter centred on her. They all agreed that John's wife could speak. John's wife greeted the people and told them the secret of their success. She began, "Whenever my husband comes home from work on his pay day, he gives me the whole of the salary." At that, the people roared with laughter, wondering how the man could be so stupid.

"He gives you the whole salary, and what do you do with it?" they chorused.

"My mother taught me something when I was growing up, and that was what I did with it," she replied. "I have envelopes for everything we do: feeding, offering, clothes, school fees, transportation, building project, savings, and more. Each time he brought his pay check, I divided the money and put some in each of the envelopes. I ensured that there was no leftover. If for any reason the money for one particular area was not enough, and it was something that needed to be attended to (perhaps the children were suddenly asked to buy a particular book and the money budgeted for books was not enough), I would take from John's transport money. John would have to walk to the office for some time. He would have to walk to the office for that time so the children could have their textbook and we didn't have to borrow. We also don't touch our savings. When we had enough money for the first house, John called somebody to come and help us to build it. After building the first house, we moved into a part of it and rented out the other. The rent increased our income, and we continued to do what we had been doing. Not too long later, we had enough money to build the second and the third houses. Later, we sent one of our children to London and the other to America." Everybody rose and started applauding for her ingenuity and wisdom.

7.10 Develop a Saving Culture

It is very important for us to desire to save, even if all you have is $1,000. If you cannot save from that, you will not be able to save from a higher income. Saving is a habit that you have to desire. The power of compounding will make money grow rapidly over time. Saving requires you to be disciplined. You save once, and you continue to save. It becomes a habit after a time. It is advisable that you save between ten percent and twenty percent of whatever income you earn. You can gradually increase the percentage over time. You would be amazed at the amount you will have saved as time goes on.

7.11 Believe

What you believe in is very important in wealth creation. In my early years, I believed in idol worshipping until I was introduced to Christianity. Initially, I would go to church in the morning, and in the evening, I would continue with the idol worshipping. We were mixing the two belief systems until some people came and said that we should become free thinkers. I became a free thinker before I was properly introduced to Christ. I have since followed Christ, and it is working for me. I have introduced Him to my children and many others. I recommend Him to you because He will work for you too.

If you don't have what you believe in, people will introduce you to something that could damage your life. You will be moving from one faith to the other, or you will come up with many faiths without being sure of what is the real thing that will save you from eternal condemnation and punishment.

7.12 Renew Yourself Spiritually

To create wealth, you need to have a relationship with God. He created everything and everyone and has plans for everyone. You must know that God wants you to have wealth and to be comfortable. He desires that you prosper in all that you do. God can lead you by dropping wealth-creation ideas in your mind. Do you believe in prayer? Prayer is the foundation for ensuring success and overcoming anxiety. Prayer is powerful. The person who prays is stronger than the person who has a knife and power. If you can pray, then nothing will be difficult for you.

7.13 Be Generous Towards God and Man

It is important that you are generous towards God. Recognize Him as the source of all that you have and will ever have. See yourself as a steward to God. Every time you earn something, give at least ten percent of it to God. This is called tithing. This is very important. You must pay your tithe so that God can pour out a blessing for you that your barn cannot contain. Generosity towards man includes the poor in the society and charity programmes. As you give generously of yourself and your money, you will receive generously too. It may not be from where you gave, but you will receive it. It is good to give to God and others

Related Story: And the Devourer Came

Sometime ago, we got a job in my company for which we were paid thirty percent in advance. I decided that when we were paid the next amount, I would pay God His own. So I finished using the money to continue the work, and I spent some. Next, we were paid thirty percent again; I did not give my ten percent to God at this stage. I noticed that my business was not growing. My brother heard that I was becoming sick, so he came to me and asked what I wanted. He said that he was sure it was a money problem. I told him I needed a little money to complete a job. He gave me the money. I removed ten percent for tithe. I was left with 90% of the sum. With that money, I was able to complete the job, and we were given another job thereafter.

I learned my lesson from that time to pay my tithes and offerings. God's law says give, and it shall be given unto you. Good measure pressed down and shaken together and running over shall men give to your bosom. Farmers know this principle well. They know that if you don't give or sow seeds, you will not reap. They know that if you don't put a mango seed into the soil, you won't get a mango tree. Another thing about giving is that God wants you to do so cheerfully and not grudgingly. God will reward you when you give without grudging. Malachi 3: 10 (KJV) says, "Bring ye all tithes into the store house that there may be meat in mine house and prove me now herewith saith the LORD of Host if I will not open you the windows of heaven and pour you out a blessing that there shall be no room enough to receive it."

On one occasion, I went to England. In the church, we were asked to give £1,000 and to bring it to the altar. That was and it is a lot of money, but I gave all the same. Later, I went to see a client of mine who said to me, "You did something for us, and we want to pay you. We have been looking for you." The client gave me three times the money I sowed. I have learned by experience that the word of God is true.

Furthermore, people don't tithe rightly. When the tithe is supposed to be $1,000 and you give $100, you have not obeyed. You have not paid the correct amount. Don't short-change God.

When it comes to special pledges and funds, make your contribution to them if you can. It is not by force. Where I live, a church was about to be built. Money was needed, and I gave. I prayed to God that the day that church would be opened my house would be opened too. God started to bless me, and the work on my building commenced and continued steadily. Miraculously, the same day that the general overseer of the church came to commission the church was the same day my house was dedicated and opened for use. They opened the church in the morning and opened my house in the evening.

Whenever there is a special fund, be part of it. You may not have the money, but God will help you. Give donations. Nobody is forcing you, but the peace of God will guide you. Give along the way when you meet people. Be generous towards others. When you give, you are giving to God. He will be happy. It is in situations like these that you are proven.

You must give to the servants of God. Give to pastors. Honour them. I have this pastor friend. Whenever I give to him, people bless me. I get jobs and other things. It is important to give to them. We must be generous towards God and towards man.

7.14 Have a Strategic Life Plan

The next thing is that you must determine your stage in life. Life is in stages. From age one to eighteen, you may not have too much control of your time. You are still under the control of your parents, but you look forward to what you want to be and the profession you want to be in. For some people, it is after high school that their career will start. From that time, you are expected to plan what will happen by the time you retire. Use the following questions to help you prepare your strategic life plan.

- What will you do?
- Where will you be?
- When are you going to marry?

- How many children will you want to have?
- Where do you want to live?
- Do you want to go back to the village you are from?
- Do you want to live in the same country or state or another?
- Do you want to have dual citizenship?
- What educational level do you want to attain?
- What aspirations do you have for your children?
- How far do you want your children to go in their education?

The above questions are not exhaustive. You are expected to provide answers to these questions. Write down your answers so that you don't forget.

Related Story: My Son

One day, I told one of my children to sit down so we could determine a ten-year plan for him. He did the writing himself. He wanted to go abroad after finishing his first degree and so on. He wrote everything down, and I kept reminding him of the plan. Today, he has accomplished a substantial part of it. One of his goals was that he would have more than a first degree. He has a second degree, even though he changed his mind on the course to become a pastor. He decided to go back to school to do another degree in theology, and he earned first class honours. I told him that he should marry around a particular age, and God helped him around that period. He married a beautiful, caring woman. Another goal was that he would write a book. He has written a book, and I am still asking him to write more. Although ten years have passed, that plan is still there, acting as a compass. If a person has a plan, he will not wander about. Such a person does not waste time or other resources. He sees opportunities, follows them, and grabs them. It is very important to plan your life because if you don't plan your life, you will waste it. With a plan in place, you won't waste time with frivolities.

7.15 Avoid Greed

Let there be contentment in you. Whatever God has given you, be grateful to God for it, and let God know that you are grateful. Don't compare yourself with others. Contentment will give you peace of mind and prevent all the pain that greed brings.

Avoid any programme or proposal that says you will get rich quick. Such promises are scams or near scams, which will attract a greedy heart. Wealth building is a gradual process. Step by step, you build your character and create your wealth. Do not allow greed to lead to doing illegal things that will violate the laws of humanity and God. Avoid greedy tendencies.

7.16 Be Humble

Develop a humble spirit and be meek. Riches, honour, and life are in humility and the fear of the Lord. Don't let pride deprive you of your progress. Always humble yourself. In humility, people will want to help you. I know one rich man who, when he meets you and wants to get something from you, will be so humble that you will not be able to turn him down. He does not show any form of arrogance. Steadily, he has built up a great wealth for himself and children. "By humility and the fear of the Lord are riches, honour and life." (Proverbs 22: 4, KJV.)

Pride brings destruction. Do not let your pride deprive you of your blessings. When you are arrogant, people will not want to help you, so you must humble yourself. Don't let money make you arrogant. Don't insult your workers, and don't insult the people who are close to you. In humility, create and accumulate wealth. Teach children to be humble and be an example unto them.

7.17 Avoid Evil and Wickedness

Run away from things and people who make you wicked. Don't go into wickedness. Don't bring people down to make money. If you do, even if it works for you initially, it won't last for long. Be fair to all, and do no evil. Run away from evil things and those who are evil and wicked.

7.18 Look for Creative Ways to Earn Extra Income

You must look for creative ways to earn extra income. Think of what you can do after work. Is there anybody you can work for? Is there anywhere you can work on some or all weekends? For instance, in our academy, we organize classes for people during the weekend. You can teach there and earn extra money. You can write lecture notes from your house. These are ways of earning something extra. You can create a laboratory for people in your house and help them test things and give them the results. Or you can have a cold room where you help people store things, and they will pay you. Look for ways to earn any extra income. Let there be more than one source of income for yourself. Never be satisfied with one source.

For example, my wife, who is the executive director of our academy, has extra jobs. She is a music minister, an author, a presenter, and a trainer. Look inward: What are your talents? Develop them. What is your hobby? How can you turn it into a source of income? Find a way to generate more income, and save part of the money generated.

7.19 Get Yourself Out of Debt.

There is a story of a woman who borrowed a dress to attend a function. She was a good dancer. When she got there, she started dancing very well. Suddenly, the person who lent her the dress saw her and said, "Ah, do you want to tear my dress?" She was so embarrassed that she could not raise her head. That is what happens when you don't live within your means. Get out of debt. Debt is not good. Don't borrow money to massage your ego. Don't borrow money for consumption. Pay up your debts, and be free. Live within your income.

A brother stood as a surety for a couple, and the couple lost the borrowed money. When the bank could not get the money from the couple, the bankers came for the brother, and he had to pay through a debt-settlement plan. Be careful of being a surety for people. You may not borrow, but if you stand as a surety, you are putting yourself up for debt if the borrower defaults.

7.20 Change the Way You Think

To create wealth, you must change the way you think. Many people don't know that wealth comes from the mind. Many people think that wealth creation is a function of luck or hard work. Neither is the case. Rather, as man thinks in his heart, so is he. "For as he thinketh in his heart, so is he: Eat and drink he says to thee; but his heart is not with thee." (Proverbs 23: 7, KJV.) You must programme your mind to be a rich man. You must programme yourself to be self-sufficient. That is why you see someone who has straight A's in the university being employed by another who managed to simply pass his degree examinations through the same university. And he will be complaining. While the latter has become a success in the University of Life, the former is still struggling.

You have to reprogramme your mind. You must get rid of financial limitation mentality. By that, I mean a mentality where you think that you can't buy something or that something is beyond you. Rather, say to yourself that you can buy it later. You will find that you will buy it sooner or later if you do not doubt your ability to do so. What are you thinking about yourself? Are you thinking you are small and that some people are big? No. You are big. The bigger you want to be, the bigger you will be. The smaller you think, the smaller you are. This can be illustrated with the story of the spies sent by Moses to

Canaan. When they came back, they said they were like grasshoppers in their own sight.

They said that the land was a fertile land, but the people there were giants. Two of them said to stop that mentality because they were able. God would help us, and they would take over the land. Only those two people entered the Promised Land. The remaining ten died before they got there.

You must think in line with what God tells you. "There is nothing that is too difficult for me. God will help me." There is nothing too difficult for you. Take the word of God and believe that He will do what He promises. You must see yourself as a lender, not a borrower. You will be a lender and not a borrower if you follow the right principles and adopt them with the right attitude.

Related Story: Myself

I didn't know Jesus Christ until I was forty-two years old. Before I gave my life to Christ, I borrowed money to build a paper-processing factory. My uncle gave me the land to build the factory on. One day, my uncle came and said he wanted to be a shareholder in the business. I refused. I did not realize that I had offended him. He began to send people after me. I started suffering in the business, and I had borrowed money to start the business. With interest, that loan became about five times the amount I borrowed, and I did not have the money to repay it.

Since I could not pay it back, my creditors asked for one of the houses I had used as a surety. It was in this process that I became born again. I asked God to make me a lender and not a borrower.

I gave the machines I was using in my factory to a ministry that had literature as a major part of its work. My friends laughed at me and asked how I could give my machines to a ministry when I was in debt. I told them what God said about giving. "Give and it shall be given unto you; good measure, pressed down, and shaken together, and running over, and for with the same measure that ye mete withal it shall be measured to you again." (Luke 6: 38, KJV.)

After I gave away the machines, I said, "I have given, God. Do your part."

One day, I went to the bank and met somebody I had met before. He informed me that the bank could give a waiver and that I should go see the managing director. He said that all I needed to do was send in an application for a waiver. On leaving there, I met a friend who asked me whether I knew that the managing director was a member of our fellowship.- The Full Gospel Business Men's Fellowship International. He advised me to simply share my story with the managing director instead of going through the waiver process. I did as my friend suggested, and indeed, I got a waiver.

The word of God says that we should be lenders and not borrowers. Think of success, and He will support you. A man named Isaac sowed in the same land that was experiencing famine, and he reaped in the same year one-hundred fold. Genesis 26: 12 (KJV) says, "Then Isaac sowed in that year and received in the same year hundred folds: and the Lord blessed him."

He went forward and became very great until people began to envy him. This should also be part of our story: Change your thinking. If you think you cannot, surely you cannot. If you think you can, you will be amazed that you will. God says that all those who labour and are heavily laden should come to Him and He will give them rest. Matthew 11: 28 (KJV) says, "Come unto me, all ye that labour and are heavy laden, and I will give you rest."

He will give you rest from financial difficulty. But you must believe that God can help you. You can do all things through Christ who strengthens you (Philippians 4: 13, KJV).

When you have financial difficulty, encourage yourself in the Lord. David did this after his wives and children were taken from him, and he recovered all (1 Samuel 30: 18, KJV). You will recover everything that was taken from you. Just believe.

Thinking Strategy

This is about how to think. The way you think will affect your achievement and results. You should consider three aspects of thinking: proactive thinking, creative thinking, and replicative thinking.

Proactive Thinking

The first strategy is proactive thinking. You must be proactive in your thought process. You must always think ahead. You must continuously ask yourself a number of questions. How do I get where I hope to get to? Who do I need to get me there? What are the resources I need to get there? What other things do I need to do to get me there? You have to think of success even before you see the success. Think of wealth before you create the wealth. Creating wealth starts from the mind. Your thinking is crucial to your success.

Creative Thinking

To create wealth, you need creative thinking. You must think creatively. A thing is created twice: in the mind when it is visualized and then when it becomes a reality. This is best illustrated in the building of a house. The architect visualizes it in his mind and sketches the mental picture of the house on a piece of paper. Sometimes, the architect produces a prototype (called a model) of the house. These allow the owner to see what the house would look like. The second creation occurs when the house is actually built. Now, you can see and enter the rooms in the house. The house is a reality. To create wealth, you must be able to think of a new and better way of doing an existing thing or how to improve on what others have done. Better still; think about what others have not done before. You must think of new twists in an old process. Be creative. If you do something a certain way now, try another way next time.

Replicative Thinking

Another strategy you need to create wealth is replicative thinking. This refers to the ability to replicate what is happening elsewhere. For example, if people are doing something in London, you must ask yourself whether it is possible to do that same thing in Johannesburg or New Delhi. You can also ask yourself whether you can add a little thing to it when taking it to Johannesburg or New Delhi. After all, there are cultural and environmental differences among the three cities. There is no need to reinvent the process if someone has already done it and it is working well. Think of replicating the same process or product or service elsewhere.

7.21 Never Stop Investing

It is through investment that more money than you can consume is generated. It's accumulation that yields wealth. You must not stop investing. A man named Isaac invested and kept investing. He dug a well, and some people came and covered it. He dug another one, and the people struggled with him. He kept doing it until they stopped. "And he removed from thence and digged another well; and for that they strove not: and he called the name of it Rehoboth; and he said, for now the LORD hath made room for us and we shall be fruitful in the land." (Genesis 26: 22, KJV).

You must embrace investment, and you must do it continuously. Cast your bread in the morning, and in the evening, withhold not. You don't know which one will do well.

It is those who don't invest who don't have wealth. If you want to be rich, you should be looking for money to invest, not to consume. It is the money you invest that will yield the money you will consume. It is a simple process, but many people fail to grab it. Do not fail to learn to save and invest whatever you have saved.

7.22 Prepare Your Mind for Success

It is very important that you be prepared for success in the accumulation of wealth. If you are not prepared, you will not be motivated to continue when you meet the storm and challenges of life. When difficulties come and it seems as if there is no way forward, a prepared mind will not give up easily. The mind is powerful. It is available for every person to use, but most people do not make use of their mind as they should. There are many books on the mind. Try to read some of them and develop your mind as an instrument for accomplishing great success in life. "For as he thinketh in his heart so is he: eat and drink saith he to thee but his heart is not with thee." (Proverbs 23: 7, KJV). If you think success, you will meet with success. If you think failure, you will meet with failure. Think wealthy, and grow rich. Say whatever the mind conceives. If you can conceive it in your mind that you will become wealthy, you can achieve it. The techniques you will use and the path to follow will be made available to you. If you want to be rich and prosperous, start thinking about prosperity and wealth. Listen to podcasts, CDs, and cassettes that will motivate you to success. Fill your mind with successful thoughts and have a plan for your life. Be focused and positive. You do not need to be rich to prepare a wealth-achievement plan. No matter your present financial level, you can start to see yourself coming out of financial failure into a life of wealth and prosperity.

7.23 Get Knowledge and Make Money

Accumulation of wealth is not limited to those who are holders of college degrees or professional qualifications. Many wealthy people have never attended the university, but they are rich and have employed best brains from the university to work for them. Lack of education is not a barrier to wealth creation. If you have little education, do not worry. You can learn what is required to be wealthy. It is a matter of changes in your lifestyle coupled with determination, hard work, and dedication.

Information is very essential for wealth creation. You need to know what you need and how to get it. After acquiring the information, how will you use it? You have to acquire knowledge. You do this by reading books. It is important to read and study. If you want health, read books about health. Study to acquire knowledge about health. If you want to acquire wealth, study about wealth. Glean knowledge about those who are rich and how they got there and remained rich. As much as possible, seek out knowledge about wealth creation. You can attend seminars, conferences, or workshops to improve your knowledge. The Internet has made it easy for information and knowledge about anything to be obtained by just a click of the button. There are many groups online that share information on various topics and areas of life. You can join any of them, especially those relating to wealth creation, business management, and personal and success strategies. They are often free to join, and you can leave the group anytime you want without any restrictions. Invest in yourself continuously. Develop and acquire knowledge and improve your potential.

Read and Study the Word of God

The Bible contains many verses that give directions about life and the world. Everything you want to know about business is contained in the Bible. The rich and the poor alike can learn great lessons from the Bible.

Use the Bible to guide you on your journey to wealth creation. You will understand. There are time-tested principles for success and wealth creation. More importantly, you will know the commands of God. Your life on earth and thereafter will be better and more assured.

7.24 Establish Your Own Business

If well-managed, a business will enable you to generate profits. Accumulation of wealth will result from continuous profit making and retention of part of the profits for expansion of the business.

In addition to wealth accumulation, the benefits of establishing your own business will include:

- Freedom (the freedom to work how and when you want as well as the freedom to create your life and make it enjoyable and rewarding)
- Self-esteem
- Job security through self-employment
- Financial reward
- The power to impact in the community and even the nation
- Satisfaction with what you are doing.

❖ Critical Issues to Consider Before Starting A Business

There are three issues to consider here: managerial skills, technical skills, and business plan.

o **Managerial Skills**

These are skills that have to do with the effective allocation of resources (both human and material) that will enable you achieve your goal. They are essential to the running of an enterprise.

This category has often been overlooked, especially by those who have vocational competence. They think that because they know the art of the vocation that business is possible. However, one has to learn how to run the business enterprise itself. Just because you know how to make good clothes doesn't automatically mean you will be a successful dressmaker. Learn how to run a business before putting your technical skills of good dressmaking into use. This will guarantee success and growth of the business.

> Some of the major business skills you will learn are marketing and customer care.
>
> Bookkeeping, accounting, basic records and systems organization are important. You will also want to know about human resources, including recruitment, training, and development. Profit planning for success and growth is also imperative.

o **Technical Skills**

This is the knowledge of the specific line of business you want to start. In other words, these technical skills are the practical abilities you need to produce the product or provide the service of your business.

The more you know about your business, the easier it will be for you to avoid making mistakes. You will know the market, competitors, and suppliers. Technical skills can be acquired through continuous learning and practice.

o **Business Plan**

A business plan is the map that shows a person where he is going. It contains the complete layout of the business, including the input and expectations of the owner. It is a picture of what you want the business to look like and how it will be operated.

Establishing your own business, if properly run, you will accelerate your wealth accumulation. You will have wealth to leave to your children.

CHAPTER 8

Rules for Wealth to Guide Parents and Their Children

If you want your children to create wealth and be wealthy, it is important for you to raise the children according to principles that have worked in the lives of others. It is a mistake to pamper your children with wealth. Failure to teach them financial and wealth principles may leave you with regrets.

Pampered children will squander the wealth you leave for them. They will become ridiculed and a source of poverty in your family. While you are alive, some of such children may become liabilities to be carried by you in your old age. Peace of mind and joy will be lost because of the failure and financial torments of such children. It is better to do something now. You will be happy, and your children will maintain and increase the wealth you leave for them. According to Thomas Stanley and William D. Danko, in their book "The Millionaire Next Door", the following valuable information has been gathered from affluent parents who have successful children. You can learn from them.

8.0 Rule 1

Make sure you do not tell your children that you are rich and wealthy

8.1 Rule 2

Irrespective of the magnitude of your wealth. Make sure you teach your children the principles of wealth creation which includes financial discipline and prudent management of resources.

8.2 Rule 3

Note that you are not to compete with your children. No comparison of your achievement with theirs.

8.3 Rule 4

Stay clear of the family matters of your children, especially the adult children. Don't complicate their lives by your interference which they don't want in any case. They may make mistakes from which they will learn in life.

8.4 Rule 5

It is not wise to discuss what gifts or inheritance you will give to your children and grandchildren. Some of the children may become lazy and unmotivated to work for their own wealth.

8.5 Rule 6

Encourage each child to settle into the profession or vocation of his or her choice, but don't reveal to them your actions and provision for their future.

8.6 Rule 7

Encourage each child to focus on success and achievement. Paint for them the virtues of success. Let them know that it is easy to consume resources but very difficult to accumulate resources.

8.7 Rule 8

Do not make the mistake of rewarding your underachieving children. The children will not perform at the same level. Some will be excellent while some may underperform. Your duty is to motivate every child. No favouritism or pampering of underachievers,

8.8 Rule 9

Show love to all your children. Anytime you give cash or a gift, let it be out of love and not because of pressure, blackmail, or coercion. Be firm, loving and assuring.

8.9 Rule 10

Convince your children that money is not the most important and valuable thing in life. Let them know that many things are important than money. Health is wealth. Love and a good companionship are greater than money. Honesty, integrity, and good character are very important and let your children know all these and be an example unto them.

8.10 Rule 11

Train your children to respect and honour God. Ephesians 6: 4 (KJV) says, "And ye fathers provoke not your children to wrath. But bring them up in the nurture and admonition of the LORD."

Man cannot live by bread alone. Matthew 4: 4 (KJV), "But he answered and said that man shall not live by bread alone but by every word that proceedeth out of the mouth of God." God is the creator of heaven and earth. The power of God is greater than the power of man. If your children can obey and serve God, they will live their days in prosperity and their years in pleasure and joy. Job 36: 11 (KJV) says, "If they obey and serve him, they shall spend their days in prosperity, and their years in pleasure."

8.11 Rule 12

Teach your children the way they should go, and when they grow up, they will not depart from what you have thought them (Proverbs 22: 6). Teach them about savings and investment when they are young. Make them to know the importance of savings over consumption. Let them know that savings and investment are the main source of wealth. Teach them to know that each of them has been created to excel and create wealth. God created each of them to be a wealth builder. They should not be engaged in wasting of resources or hyperconsumption of resources to show a high life status. This is wasteful and against the rules of wealth creation. Frugality is the watchword that should govern their pattern.

8.12 Rule 13

To be frugal means to show economy and prudence in the use of resources. This should be imbibed by your children because being frugal is a crucial aspect of wealth building.

8.13 Rule 14

Don't fund your children's education from your retirement kitty. Have a separate fund for it.

CHAPTER 9

How to Stay Wealthy

Health is wealth goes a general axiom; part of the reason for wealth accumulation is to live in sound health while encouraging others about how to live a fulfilled life. To make money don't lose your health. Your health is very important. After accumulating wealth, you have to remain rich and wealthy including good health physically and spiritually. There are principles you can follow to ensure that your wealth does not disappear or diminish before you know it. Go through the principles and make use of them as you continue to create and accumulate wealth.

9.0 You Need Financial Health Check

If you want to stay wealthy, you need regular financial health check. It is you who carries out the check at a regular time (for example, every Friday or Saturday). You could make it every month, but it is better for you to have a firm grip on your financial situation. The earlier you are aware of any changes, the better it will be for you to react and make necessary changes. What follows is what the financial health check should include.

A reconciliation of your bank accounts, both business and personal. If you are in business and cannot do the reconciliation, engage the services of an accountant to help you do it regularly. The more often it is done, the better and easier it is.

Other things to check include:

- A list of your creditors (those you owe money)
- A list of your debtors (those who owe you)
- Credit card balances (reconcile using receipts)
- Unpresented cheques (cheques you have issued but have not been presented to the bank for payment)
- Uncredited items (money paid into the bank that is not yet credited by the bank)
- Future income available for you and when you ought to receive it
- Any major expenses that will soon fall due
- Any standing orders you might have given to the bank (the review will show whether you need to cancel or reduce the amount of the order)
- Pension contributions and statements.
- Investments (items such as shares, bonds, money market investments, overdrafts loans, credit lines, and leases should be checked as part of your regular financial health check)

There is much to be gained by conducting a regular financial check.

- You will block any leakages that are existing in your wealth-accumulation system.
- Things will not go drastically wrong before your discovering them.
- You will be able to take measures should you discover that things are not going as you expected or if there are omissions.
- If you are able to focus on a regular financial health check, it will keep you prosperous, and your wealth creation plan will remain on course.

9.1 Mentorship

It is of great advantage for you to supplement your knowledge and experience with the vast knowledge and experience of other people. You cannot know everything. Choose mentors who have accumulated wealth through legitimate and morally acceptable means. Do not choose those who became wealthy through inheritance, lottery, corruption or illegality. You can choose one or more mentors in the area of finance and other mentors for other areas of your life (for example, spiritual or professional mentors). There are multiple benefits of a financial mentor.

- They bring you varied and tested principles for success in financial matters.
- They help you leverage on your mentor's wide experience to improve your own experience and decision-making process.
- They will stand as avenues to present and test the reality of your ideas. It will task you to prove the feasibility and viability of your projects and money-making ideas.
- They will connect you to their network and gather information for you concerning your ideas or project.

You need mentors. The earlier you can approach one or two people who you like and have proven, the better it will be for you on your journey to wealth accumulation.

9.2 Never Try to Get Wealthy Quickly

Do not be so greedy that you will take steps to get your wealth multiplied overnight through a get-rich-quick plan. If you get rich quickly through a lottery or any luck-dependent programme, the tendency is for the wealth to disappear quickly – just the way it came.

There are many people around proposing business opportunities that will guarantee quick returns and abundance of wealth. These people have designed the programmes for those who will not wait to make wealth through a genuine, slow-and-steady means.

It is better to create wealth slowly. Be careful so that you do not lose all that you have spent years to accumulate overnight.

A man retired from his well-paid job and was paid a lump sum of $500,000. A group of young people came and presented the man with a plan that would guarantee him a 200% returns on his investment every year. The plan was limited to the stock market.

The $500,000 was invested with the finance guide. Two years later, the investment was gone. No capital, bonus, or profits could be recovered.

Gambling is another area where people lose money and forfeit their wealth-accumulation opportunities. Do not engage yourself in gambling of any type. It is better for you to build various streams of income gradually and have a solid foundation upon which you can gradually and steadily build wealth.

9.3 Always Shop Around and Negotiate Before Buying

It is possible to purchase the same goods of the same quality for different prices if you purchase from different sellers. Develop the habit of getting quotes from three or more shops before you make a purchase. Even if you have the money, it is not to your advantage to throw away the money because you cannot shop around.

In addition to shopping around, negotiate the price. After getting quotes from three people or organizations, try to negotiate the price and terms of the purchase. You cannot get from the sellers what you want as you want it unless you negotiate and make them know that you have the option of going somewhere else. A friend of mine who is relatively wealthy and in the real estate and trading industry would start any negotiation by cutting the quoted price by half and insisting on removal of the conditions he did not like. He will do the same thing with many sellers before comparing quality, price, delivery, and other terms.

He shops around and loves doing so. I have learned from him. I do the same thing, though not with the same dexterity. Always shop around before you make the purchase. Negotiate the price and terms to reduce what money will flow out from you; be conscious that you are receiving value for the money you are spending. You need to teach your children to spend wisely as you practice the art of shopping around.

9.4 Control Your Expenses

Your current level of wealth was accumulated by you or handed over to you via an inheritance. You and those who started the wealth accumulation must have been conscious of the need to control expenses. Impulsive buying must be controlled. Otherwise, no wealth will be created. To stay wealthy, this principle of controlling expenses must be intensified. Before you buy anything, you have to ask yourself whether the purchase is necessary or if it can be delayed. Is it worth it? Can you make do with something you already have? What value will it add to your earning capacity? Your answer to these questions will guide you in buying. You may have the money, but you must control the spending. Spending money is much easier than earning money.

9.5 Avoid Flaunting of Wealth

One other thing that you need to avoid is flaunting of your wealth. As you become wealthy, try to keep your display of wealth to the barest level. The things you are buying today to show that you have arrived will soon become old and work much less efficiently than the amount at which you purchased it. Also, a new edition or model will soon come out. To satisfy your instinct for showing off, you will acquire the new model. Before you know it, instead of generating more wealth, the rate of wealth generation will be falling. If there is any unexpected distortion to your income source, you may find that your wealth disappears quickly. Flaunting of wealth also has a negative side that you should consider. It may attract robbers and negative publicity which may affect the safety of your life as well as that of your loved ones. Keep a low profile with your wealth, and manage it well.

9.6 Remember the Tax Man

As you become wealthy, you will become a target for the tax man. Tax, like death, cannot be evaded permanently. Tax evasion is a criminal offence for which there are severe penalties, including fines and jail term. All the money accumulated could be wiped out by the tax man if you ignore him. It is better to set aside a portion for the tax man and pay it as soon as it is due. If you cannot handle the tax matters yourself, you can secure the services of a tax expert or a professional accountant to sort out tax liabilities.

A man told me the story of his encounter with the tax authorities. He established his business, but he was not paying the appropriate tax. He established the business in two other locations using this method of tax evasion. One day, a mere coincidence brought up his company's name in the course of tax investigations of his suppliers. Through this link, his company was traced, and a big investigation started. He was charged with fraud for which he engaged lawyers and used all his resources to fight the case. In the end, he was able to escape from fraud on a technical point, but the tax liability for which he was assessed was more than the value of all his assets. He was declared bankrupt. His case is a lesson for those who ignore or try to dodge the tax man. The repercussions could go beyond imaginable proportion. Deal with the tax man, and save yourself the heartache.

9.7 Continue to Sow Seeds for Harvest

Create more streams of income. The stream(s) that made you rich should be carefully managed, but other sources should be established.

Relying on one major stream of income is dangerous because it could cease at any time due to unforeseen circumstances. Take steps to create additional streams of income to improve your foundation of wealth accumulation.

A farmer knows that he must plant seeds so there is a crop to harvest. In the same way, you will need to sow seeds to have increases from which you will add to your accumulated wealth.

One way of sowing seed is to share your wealth with charitable and faith-based organizations. As you care for others through your wealth, you will receive increase in return for your sharing. It is a principle that you should embrace if you want to be wealthy and stay wealthy. Giving for just cause and giving to God's work will keep you wealthy. Spend from the increase you receive; there is great joy in sharing and spending for a good cause.

9.8 Keep Abreast of Technology

Technological advancement will continue, and only those who are able to keep changing will be able to optimize their potentials. Social networks connect people in every part of the world. These are great marketing sources. Portable devices like iPads and iPhones make communication easier and cheap for business across continents and nations. You cannot ignore the power of these changes. To remain wealthy, you will need to acquire and use these new devices to your advantage.

CHAPTER 10

Wealth: Daily Advice from Great Minds

I have included quotations, words of advice, and statements that can be used every day as part of the resource for creating and accumulating wealth. There are thirty-one in all, one for each day in a month. The reader is expected to pick one a day and think of how to make use of the information on the daily journey to wealth creation. I believe you will learn from the great minds who have talked, taught, and motivated others for centuries on wealth and wealth creation.

Day 1
Have a Dream

Your dream is very powerful. Nobody can quarrel with you for dreaming. Dream and dream big. Dreams are very powerful. Your dreams will motivate and guide you to push forward on the journey to wealth creation and accumulation. You can dream yourself into affluence. Dream that you are a multimillionaire. Dream that you have escaped from poverty with wealth. It will not cost anything to dream. Start dreaming now. The fact that you had a nightmare shouldn't stop you from dreaming. Dream big and possess your possessions.

Day 2
A Poor Man's Wisdom Is Always Despised

This is an example of wisdom that greatly impressed me. There was once a small city with only a few people in it. A powerful king came against it, surrounded it, and brought a huge siege against it. There lived in that city a man poor but wise, and he saved the city with his wisdom. However, nobody remembered that poor man. Wisdom is better than strength, but the poor man's wisdom was despised and his words are no longer headed (Ecclesiastes 9: 13–16, NKJV).

If you are poor and unsuccessful, no one will have regard for your wisdom. People will ask why you aren't successful with your wisdom. Therefore, you need wisdom, and you also need to build riches and wealth.

Day 3
God Gives Wealth

"But thou shall remember the Lord thy God: for it is He that giveth thee power to get wealth that, he may establish his covenant which he swore unto thy fathers, as it is this day." (Deuteronomy 8: 18, KJV).

Every day of your life, you must pray and worship God. God is your maker. Your maker is the creator of heaven and earth. He gives you the power to make wealth, and he keeps you alive. Remember Him as you wake every day. Before you go to sleep, thank Him for the benefits given to you.

Day 4
The Lord Blesses All the Time

"The Lord shall open unto thee his good treasure, the heavens to give rain unto thy land in his season, and to bless all the works of thy hand: and thou shall lend unto many nations and thou shall not borrow." (Deuteronomy 28: 12, KJV).

You live in a universe where there is unlimited abundance. There is enough for you and everybody on earth. The provider of all resources is with you always. He has promised to make you live in abundance. Remember that no matter where you are now, God will make a way for you by opening His bounty to you. Be of good courage. There is enough for you

Day 5
The Key to Financial Goals

Wealth-creation planning is the key to achieving all your financial goals, including retirement. Income and wealth are not the same. Income is the inflow of earnings. It is the means to achieving wealth, but it is not wealth itself. You may earn a high income but still be poor. You need to save regularly and invest your savings wisely. If you spend all or most of what you earn, you will not be rich. You must learn to save for yourself and your loved ones to create wealth.

Day 6
It Is Simple to Become Wealthy

The starting point for becoming rich is to have a desire to be wealthy. If you have the desire, you will be ready to discipline yourself to formulate and implement a wealth-creation plan. A burning desire to be rich will make you to monitor the progress on your journey of wealth creation. You will not fall off track in the process. It will be your motivating factor to continue with greater enthusiasm.

Day 7
Desire Is Important for Wealth Creation

If you want to be rich, it does not require any spectacular effort. The process is simple. Save at least ten percent of your income. The next step is to invest carefully what you have saved. Decide whether you want to be rich. Save and invest wisely on a regular basis, and you will become rich.

It is desire rather than exceptional intelligence or ability that is the most important element in wealth creation. Desire is allied to careful planning, and with a little extra effort, the results are marvellous to behold. If you ally desire to careful planning and diligent effort, the results will be outstanding. Strong desire with committed efforts will bring extraordinary results

Day 8
Aim High

Think big. Aim high. Set goals for your wealth destination. Write down your plan. Do not be afraid to aim high. Do not limit God. God is unlimited. Do not limit yourself. Believe you can achieve great things through the power of God. Set time limits to achieve each aspect of your goal. Look at your goal every day, and present it to God. Monitor your progress. Be certain that you will achieve the goals if you are clear about what you want to achieve and you are committed to make the goals become reality

Day 9
Cash Shortage as an Opportunity

Are you experiencing cash shortage? This is a sign that you need to review your income-earning capacity and spending patterns. It is an opportunity to determine whether you should look for other ways to earn more income. You can be engaged in part-time work or start a small business. It is important for you to have more than one stream of income. Make sure that you have taken all opportunities available for you to earn more. In addition, review your expenditures. Where is the money going? Remove unnecessary expenses, and add the amount so reduced to your savings account. It is a good strategy to increase your earning capacity while reducing your expenses. Unnecessary expenses should be eliminated.

It is necessary for you to earn income from which you can create wealth. Start from any level of income. It will grow, and you can always add more sources from which you can earn regular income. If you have no job and you are not doing anything about starting a business or a vocation, you cannot create wealth. You are already in the realm of poverty. You need to earn in order to save. From your savings, you will invest and continue the process.

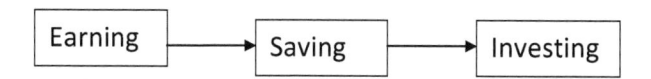

```
Earning → Saving → Investing
```

One day, you will be very rich and wealthy. Earn income, and save part of what you earn regularly. Finally, invest from what you have saved. You are on your way to great wealth and financial freedom.

Day 10
Don't Spend Everything You Earn

You should spend less than you earn. If you spend more than you are earning, you will be in debt. It means you are eating your future now. Your future will be bitter and full of lack and embarrassment. Earn more and spend less. You have to make changes in how you spend. You have to eliminate or reduce all unnecessary expenditures.

Day 11
Saving May Seem Difficult

People say it is difficult to save. They complain that what they earn is so small that they have nothing left to save. However, it is not true that you cannot save. What is difficult is how to start saving. Saving requires discipline. If you have the desire to be rich, then you must develop the discipline to save regularly. Why do you save money? It may be to cater to the unexpected or to meet long-term expectations. Perhaps you want to save for your retirement. No matter the aim, you need discipline. You must start to save immediately. If you don't start to save now, you are jeopardizing your desire to create wealth for a better future.

Day 12
Practical Ways to Manage Your Money

a. Develop new habits to save; be disciplined.
b. Avoid consumer debt.
c. Start and fund a retirement plan.
d. Arrange to pay off your mortgage.
e. Find small ways to save money.

- Reuse paper clips.
- Make sure you switch off the light when you are leaving the room.
- Buy a quality used car rather than a new one.

f. Ask questions before buying any product or service.

- Do I really need it?
- Can I say it is worth the price I am paying for it?
- Is there a substitute?
- Can I afford it at this time?

g. Replace a monetary payment with nonmonetary resources (time and energy, for example).
h. Choose the best health insurance available.
i. Think long term and always choose quality above price.
j. Understand the power of compounding and interest.
k. Avoid credit as much as possible.
l. Understand inflation and how it affects you.
m. Manage and preserve your assets.
n. Start saving when you are young, and continue the habit.
o. Learn to invest, and make use of experts to guide you.

Day 13
Tips on How to Save Regularly

- Determine how much you are going to save. Ideally, let it be at least ten percent of your income. Discipline yourself to save regularly.
- Restrain yourself from holding extra cash. Hold only the cash you need.
- Avoid spending your savings at all costs. Never dip into your savings except in case of emergency. The best strategy is to cut your expenses rather than blowing your savings.
- Make use of retirement tools such as a contributory pension plan.

Day 14
You Can Succeed and Accumulate Wealth

There is no limitation to your ability to create wealth except that the limitation you create for yourself. There is abundance of opportunities waiting for the right persons to harness. If you know what you want and you follow the right principles, you will achieve success beyond your imagination. You will need to write down what you want and back it up with a plan. Determination and persistence are crucial to success in wealth accumulation and indeed for any attempt to achieve worthy goals. Take advantage of the supernatural power of God, which is higher than any other power in heaven or earth.

The easiest way to do so is to connect yourself to the Lord Jesus Christ and build a solid relationship with the saviour of the world. Your success will last and give you peace and joy.

Use the Internet and information technology to boost you performance

Day 15
Make a Personal Will

Part of your wealth-creation plan is making a will. It is advisable that you make a will of what inheritance you will be leaving for your loved ones.

Professionals should guide you in making the will. This is inheritance. Tax burdens can be high if you fail to make proper preparation for what you will leave as your estate. In order for your family to benefit maximally, make a will.

Day 16
The Importance of Compounding in Wealth Creation

It is important that you understand the principle of compounding. It is the principle that makes it possible to accumulate phenomenal wealth creation over a long period of time. Compounding makes you to receive interest on the money you invested, which we can call your capital. The interest earned can be added to capital. The new capital becomes the capital plus your earned interest. In the next period, interest will be charged on the new capital provided no withdrawal is made. Over time, the money will continue to grow. As long as you stay in the investment, your money will continue to grow

Day 17
Plant if you want to harvest

If you want to harvest, you must first plant the seed. What you plant is what you will reap. If you plant mangoes, you will reap mangoes. If you plant oranges, you will reap oranges. If you plant very little, your harvest will be little. To have a large harvest, you need to plant a sufficient amount of seed. The larger your planting, the greater your harvest will be. You must not eat all of your seed if you want to accumulate wealth. You will eat some, save some, and invest some. Small amounts of money saved regularly will accumulate into a large sum in the future.

Day 18
What You Confess Will Come to Pass

Never confess negatively. There is great connection between what you confess with your mouth and what comes to pass in your life. Always confess that you are rich and successful. Use your mouth to call to reality what you want to achieve in your financial life. Say to yourself that you are rich and wealthy. Believe it, and repeat it with confidence. There is death and life in power of the tongue (Proverbs 18: 21, KJV).

Harness the power of your tongue to create and accumulate wealth beyond your imagination

Day 19
Embrace Technology and Prosper

The present age is the age of brain power. Information and technology have merged to change the world and how business is done. Those who ignore technology are sentencing themselves to poverty and lack from which they may not be set free from for a long time to come. If you want to create wealth from anywhere and everywhere in the world, it is imperative that you should embrace information and technology. Your race to wealth and riches will be accelerated by the use of information technology

Day 20
Be Trusted

Whoever can be trusted with very little can be trusted with much and whoever is dishonest with very little will also be dishonest with much. If you have not been trustworthy in handling worldly wealth, who will trust you with true riches? If you have not been trustworthy with someone else's property, who will give you property of your own?

Luke 16: 10 – 13 (KJV) says, "He that is faithful in that which is least is faithful also in much: and he that is unjust in the least is unjust also in much. [11] If therefore ye have not been faithful in the unrighteous mammon, who will commit to your trust the true riches? [12] And if ye have not been faithful in that which is another man's, who shall give you that which is your own?[13] No servant can serve two masters: for either he will hate the one, and love the other; or else he will hold to the one, and despise the other. Ye cannot serve God and mammon."

Integrity is crucial for success. Be a person who can be trusted. Very few people are trustworthy. Be one of them, and you will prosper.

Day 21
Maintain Honesty with God and Man

- Be a man or a woman of good character.
- Do not entangle yourself with dishonest people for business or any association.
- Be a person who will act rightly under pressure.
- Be courageous to do the right thing and hate injustice.
- Pay your tithes promptly and accurately.
- Do not cheat God or man.
- Pay your bills promptly
- Be a trustworthy person, and let your words be kept even to a point of hurt at all times.
- Your integrity must not be in doubt.
- Don't lie to yourself.
- Be generous and full of love.
- Always acknowledge that you are a caretaker and that all you have was given to you for a purpose.

Day 22
Success Comes to the Diligent

If you want to accumulate wealth, you must be diligent.

Proverbs 22:29 (KJV) says, "Seest thou a man diligent in his business? he shall stand before kings; he shall not stand before mean men."

Millionaires are financially successful people and are diligent. There is no room for laziness. The ant, a mere insect, is an example from which you can learn. Ants have no supervisor or overseers, yet they are industrious and proactive. "Go to the ant, thou sluggard; consider her ways, and be wise." Proverbs 6: 6 – 1 (KJV).

Embrace diligence, and let it guide you to success on your journey to financial freedom.

Day 23
Plan Your Retirement

Decide when you will retire. Is there a compulsory retirement age? Plan to work towards it, or retire voluntarily before that age. Estimate how much you will need in retirement to maintain the quality of life you desire. Create a regular income and understand the retirement income you will receive. Try to understand inflation and what effects it can have on your income, especially when it is fixed. Plan for your health care in old age. Planning for retirement is very important. You must start early.

Day 24
Spiritual Instruments for the Storm

When there is a storm, you have to still the storm. You have the weapons to calm the storm. Unseen forces are available to disrupt your journey unto financial success. Use the following tools to conquer and be victorious.

- The word of God. Psalms 119: 105 (KJV) says, "Thy word is a lamp unto my feet, and a light unto my path: Let the word of God be a lamp to you to guide you and strengthen you at all time."
- Prayer. Build the unseen forces. Pray against the spirit of poverty and lack. Take authority over the situation. Ephesians 6: 12 (KJV) says, "For we wrestle not against flesh and blood, but against principalities, against powers, against the rulers of the darkness of this world, against spiritual wickedness in high places." Further, Proverbs 16: 3 says, "Commit thy works unto the LORD, and thy thoughts shall be established."
- Commit to receiving counsel. Take good counsel because without counsel, you will fail. Leverage on good counsel. Proverbs 15: 22 (KJV) says, "Without counsel purposes are disappointed: but in the multitude of counsellors they are established."

Trust God. Have faith in God. Believe in Him, and He will be with you in every situation of life. Mark 11: 22–23 KJV says, "And Jesus answering saith unto them, Have faith in God.[23] For verily I say unto you, That whosoever shall say unto this mountain, Be thou removed, and be thou cast into the sea; and shall not doubt in his heart, but shall believe that those things which he saith shall come to pass; he shall have whatsoever he saith. You are a victor and not a victim. You are more than a conqueror."

Day 25
Be Ready for Wealth Accumulation

Take steps to ensure that you are ready to create and accumulate wealth. You need to embrace discipline, accountability, and positive mental alertness. Your mind must be ready for wealth creation. It is you who determines your state of mind and controls what you allow to enter your mind. You are responsible for your performance on the journey to wealth creation. If you aim low, you will have low performance. Likewise, if you aim high, you will have high performance. Whatever you ask yourself is what you will have, be it good or poor performance.

Day 26
Generosity is Necessary for Wealth Accumulation

You must be generous towards God and towards man if you want to accumulate wealth. Look at the following scriptures and follow them. God loves a cheerful giver. Giving will energise you to become wealthy.

- Pay your tithe (Malachi 3: 9–12, KJV)

    "[9] Ye are cursed with a curse: for ye have robbed me, even this whole nation. [10] Bring ye all the tithes into the storehouse, that there may be meat in mine house, and prove me now herewith, saith the LORD of hosts, if I will not open you the windows of heaven, and pour you out a blessing, that there shall not be room enough to receive it. [11] And I will rebuke the devourer for your sakes, and he shall not destroy the fruits of your ground; neither shall your vine cast her fruit before the time in the field, saith the LORD of hosts. [12] And all nations shall call you blessed: for ye shall be a delightsome land, saith the LORD of hosts."

- Give generously (Luke 6: 38, KJV)

    "³⁸ Give, and it shall be given unto you; good measure, pressed down, and shaken together, and running over, shall men give into your bosom. For with the same measure that ye mete withal it shall be measured to you again."

- Support special pledges and funds (Psalms 126: 6, KJV)

    "⁶ He that goeth forth and weepeth, bearing precious seed, shall doubtless come again with rejoicing, bringing his sheaves with him."

- Give alms (Proverbs 19: 17, KJV)

    "¹⁷ He that hath pity upon the poor lendeth unto the LORD; and that which he hath given will he pay him again."

- Give generously and regularly to the servant of God (Galatians 6: 6–7, KJV)

    "⁶ Let him that is taught in the word communicate unto him that teacheth in all good things. ⁷ Be not deceived; God is not mocked: for whatsoever a man soweth, that shall he also reap."

- Generosity when you do not have (1 King 17:11 KJV)

    The widow gave out the little food available for her and her son to the prophet of God. She was blessed. Her son, the prophet Elijah and herself had enough supply throughout the period of the famine.

    ¹¹ And as she was going to fetch it, he called to her, and said, Bring me, I pray thee, a morsel of bread in thine hand.

    ¹² And she said, As the LORD thy God liveth, I have not a cake, but an handful of meal in a barrel, and a little oil in a cruse: and,

behold, I am gathering two sticks, that I may go in and dress it for me and my son, that we may eat it, and die.

¹³ And Elijah said unto her, Fear not; go and do as thou hast said: but make me thereof a little cake first, and bring it unto me, and after make for thee and for thy son.

¹⁴ For thus saith the LORD God of Israel, The barrel of meal shall not waste, neither shall the cruse of oil fail, until the day that the LORD sendeth rain upon the earth.

¹⁵ And she went and did according to the saying of Elijah: and she, and he, and her house, did eat many days.

Day 27
Thinking Properly

Change the way you think. "For as he thinketh in his heart so he is he." (Proverbs 23: 7 KJV)

- No more financial bondage mentality.
- No more grasshopper thinking.
- Think of what the word of God says.
- Think success and support from God.
- Replace comparison with contentment (1 Timothy 6: 6 KJV): "But godliness with contentment is great gain."
- Abundance (Joel 2: 24–26, KJV): "And the floors shall be full of wheat, and the vats shall overflow with wine and oil.²⁵ And I will restore to you the years that the locust hath eaten, the cankerworm, and the caterpillar, and the palmerworm, my great army which I sent among you.²⁶ And ye shall eat in plenty, and be satisfied, and praise the name of the LORD your God that hath dealt wondrously with you: and my people shall never be ashamed."

Your thinking is very important. It must be success thinking. Action must follow your plan and confession. You can follow the story of the woman with the issue of blood. She used the following strategy to ensure success.

Step 1: She said what she wanted (Mark 5: 24–34, KJV)

"[24] And Jesus went with him; and much people followed him, and thronged him [25] And a certain woman, which had an issue of blood twelve years, [26] And had suffered many things of many physicians, and had spent all that she had, and was nothing bettered, but rather grew worse, [27] When she had heard of Jesus, came in the press behind, and touched his garment. [28] For she said, If I may touch but his clothes, I shall be whole. [29] And straightway the fountain of her blood was dried up; and she felt in her body that she was healed of that plague. [30] And Jesus, immediately knowing in himself that virtue had gone out of him, turned him about in the press, and said, Who touched my clothes? [31] And his disciples said unto him, Thou seest the multitude thronging thee, and sayest thou, Who touched me? [32] And he looked round about to see her that had done this thing. [33] But the woman fearing and trembling, knowing what was done in her, came and fell down before him, and told him all the truth. [34] And he said unto her, Daughter, thy faith hath made thee whole; go in peace, and be whole of thy plague."

Step 2: She did what she said she would do; She touched the garment of Jesus Christ

Step 3: With strong faith and action, she received what she said she would receive; healing was received immediately

Step 4: She told the story of what happened to her. Use faith as a plug to connect to the Holy Spirit. Follow the four steps, and you will succeed all the time. You can touch the garment of Jesus Christ, and there will be solution to your problems, including financial freedom and wealth accumulation

Day 28
Inspection Is Important

If you want success, you must inspect and check regularly to ensure progress. You have to monitor performance. You must inspect what others are doing for you if you want to get what you expect. You must also inspect what you are doing yourself to determine your progress. Many people fail at the point of inspection, so they fail to achieve the goals they have set for themselves. Checking regularly should be one of the skills you should develop to ensure accumulation of wealth.

Day 29
Plan for Tax and Avoid Trouble

Ensure that you plan adequately for tax. Planning for tax is legitimate, but tax avoidance is a criminal offence that will affect wealth creation and accumulation. The government is concerned about tax so it can collect revenue for planning of government business. Use professional accountants or tax experts to save your firm from any form of sanctions and embarrassment because of tax offences.

Day 30
Think and Motivate Yourself to Success

You are on your way to wealth creation. It is a good journey and highly rewarding, but you must be thinking of success on the journey. Thinking is not enough, though: You must motivate yourself and stay motivated in order to continue on the journey without turning back when there are adversities or storms of life. To ensure that you are continuously motivated, do the following.

- Find a role model and connect with that person.
- Develop a habit of inspiring yourself (for example, through music).
- Set a personal standard and compete with yourself regularly. Revise the standard when you have achieved it. This will keep you going higher and higher.

- Enhance accountability. This will enable you to measure your performance, and if you have shared your standards or goals with a trusted person, you will have to account to this person for your performance.
- Be determined to prove someone wrong who has made a statement that you cannot do something or that you cannot achieve a certain level. Be determined to achieve that level and prove the person wrong.

Day 31
Getting Wealthy Cannot Be Late

It is never too late to start creating wealth. Age is no barrier. Desire is the starting point. Commitment on your part is crucial. You must plan for wealth creation. Your plan must be implemented. Wealth creation is a journey that you can start anytime. Many millionaires are being made every year all over the world. You can be one of them. Just be sure you are ready, and be committed

CHAPTER 11

Conclusion

In this, book I have attempted to stimulate your desire to create wealth, regardless of the amount of your current personal wealth. If you have wealth bequeathed to you, it is expected that you should increase it and hand over to generations coming after you a greater amount of wealth than what your parents and grandparents gave to you.

If you feel you do not have any wealth or that you are seriously in debt, do not be dismayed. There is hope and a brighter future for you and your loved ones. You can build wealth beyond your imagination. The strategies and lifestyles discussed in this book are available to all those who desire to create wealth. There is no discrimination or any form of restriction as to those who can beneficially develop and use the strategies. There is no limit to the amount of wealth you can create, nor is there any time limit. Age is no barrier. You can start at any time and build a tremendous amount of wealth. Put together your strategies. Make your plan and start without any further delay.

The journey of a thousand miles starts with one step and then another and another until the journey is completed. Take that first step, and you will surely achieve your goal. There is also the spiritual dimension. There is the power that is greater than you. It is available to assist you. The power of the Almighty God is sure and reliable. It will accelerate your accumulation of wealth and prosper you. A commitment to Jesus Christ will enable you enjoy the gift of God's grace in your life beyond what you already know.

I encourage you to start your journey of wealth creation today. I wish you genuine success.

Bibliography

1. Cambridge International Dictionary of English, Cambridge University Press, Low Price Edition.
2. Barna, George. The Power of Vision. Regal Books, 1992
3. Cutler, Peter. How to Increase Your Personal Wealth. Thorsons (Harper Collins Publishers, Hammersmith, London) 1992
4. Thomas, Stanley J. and Danko, D. William. The Millionaire Next Door. Longstreet Press, Newmarket Parkway, USA .1998.
5. The Layman's Guide to Retirement Planning. Outlook Publishing, Ashram, New Delhi (India) Private Ltd., 2007.
6. Stopher, Michael and Mattlin, Everett. Wealth: An Owner's Manual. Harper Business, New York, USA. 1993.
7. Brott, Richard A.. Author Unknown. Biblical Principles for Success in Personal Finance. City Christian Publishing, Portland, Oregon, USA, 2006
8. Tracy, Brian. Create Your Own Future. John Wiley & Sons Inc., New York, USA 2002.
9. Hill, Napoleon. Think and Grow Rich Action Pack. PLUME, Penguin Books New York, USA, 1990.
10. Shemin, Robert. How Come that Idiot's Rich and I'm Not? Three Rivers Press, UK. 2008.
11. Templar, Richard. The Rules of Wealth. Pearson Prentice Hall, Edinburgh Gate, Great Britain, 2007.

Made in the USA
San Bernardino, CA
09 March 2018